Paul Hattaway, a native New Zeala
Asia for most of his life. He is an e
and author of *The Heavenly Man*,
China, *Shandong* and many other b   ... wife Joy are
the founders of Asia Harvest (<www.asiaharvest.org>), which
supports thousands of indigenous missionaries and has provided
millions of Bibles to Christians throughout Asia.

Also by Paul Hattaway:

The Heavenly Man

An Asian Harvest

Operation China

China's Christian Martyrs

Shandong

GUIZHOU

The Precious Province

Paul Hattaway

First published in Great Britain in 2018
Also published in 2018 by Asia Harvest, www.asiaharvest.org

Society for Promoting Christian Knowledge
36 Causton Street
London SW1P 4ST
www.spck.org.uk

Author's agent: The Piquant Agency, 183 Platt Lane, Manchester M14 7FB, UK

British Library Cataloguing-in-Publication Data
A catalogue record for this book is available from the British Library

ISBN 978–0–281–07989–6
eBook ISBN 978–0–281–07990–2

Typeset by Fakenham Prepress Solutions, Fakenham, Norfolk, NR21 8NL
First printed in Great Britain by Jellyfish Print Solutions
Subsequently digitally reprinted in Great Britain

eBook by Fakenham Prepress Solutions, Fakenham, Norfolk, NR21 8NL

Produced on paper from sustainable forests

Guizhou

贵州

"Precious State"

Map of China showing Guizhou Province

Pronounced:	Gway-joh		
Old spelling:	Kweichow		
Population:	35,247,695 (2000)		
	34,748,556 (2010)		
	34,249,417 (2020)		
Area:	68,018 sq. miles (176,167 sq. km)		
Population density:	504 people per sq. mile (194 per sq. km)		
Capital city:	Guiyang	2,520,061	
Largest cities (2010):	Zunyi	715,148	
	Liupanshui	621,488	
	Bijie	421,342	
	Anshun	358,920	
	Xingyi	335,243	
Administrative	Prefectures:	9	
divisions:	Counties:	88	
	Towns:	1,539	
			Percent
Major ethnic	Han Chinese	21,911,687	62.2
groups (2000):	Miao	4,299,954	12.2
	Bouyei	2,798,200	7.9
	Dong	1,628,568	4.6
	Tujia	1,430,286	4.1
	Yi	843,554	2.4
	Gelao	559,041	1.6
	Shui	369,723	1.0

Contents

Contents

Foreword

Like the apostle Luke, the author of the China Chronicles is a faithful servant called by the Lord. This God-fearing man is a devout prayer warrior who studies the Bible carefully and walks in the ways of the Lord. Paul Hattaway was stirred by the Holy Spirit to record the testimonies of God's people since the gospel first reached China during the Tang Dynasty (AD 635) to the present time.

He has expertly woven little-known stories of both revival and persecution into the narrative, giving a blessed overview of the work of the Holy Spirit in my homeland.

The cross of Jesus Christ is able to save. His followers have always believed that the gospel will transform China into a nation filled with disciples who love the Lord, a nation that overflows with heaven's blessings. By faith, the Chinese Church has overcome fierce opposition to spread the good news with great zeal. Because of their sacrifices and willingness to lay down their lives, they have produced a fruitful harvest for the kingdom of God, for Jesus said, "unless a kernel of wheat falls to the ground and dies, it remains only a single seed. But if it dies, it produces many seeds" (John 12.24).

I remember in the early 1980s—when the Chinese house churches were undergoing severe persecution and many of our co-workers were imprisoned—our favorite songs at the time were "Be the Lord's Witness to the Ends of the Earth," and "Martyrs for the Lord." When we sang the words "To be a martyr for the Lord, to be a martyr for the Lord," everyone would cry out, "Lord, send me to preach the gospel! I am willing to follow you! I am willing to be a martyr to glorify your name." Praise the Lord! God's time has come, and China is experiencing a rich harvest that has grown out of the ground watered by the tears and blood of those martyrs.

I believe these books are not only a gift to the people of China, but that God will use them to inspire Christians everywhere to obey God's call. May we serve with a willing heart, eager to lay down our lives, so that the Great Commission might be completed and the gospel will reach everyone who has yet to know Jesus, the risen Savior. Hallelujah! I believe this gospel of salvation will be preached to the ends of the earth, even back to Jerusalem, before the blessed return of our Lord. Amen.

A servant of God,
Brother Yun ("The Heavenly Man")

Preface

Over many years and generations, the followers of Jesus in China have set their hearts to be the witnesses of Christ to the nation. Many have paid a great price for their ministry, and the brutal persecutions they have endured for the faith have often been unimaginable.

The Bible commands all believers to "Go into all the world and preach the gospel to all creation" (Mark 16.15). Many foreign missionaries responded to this command in the past, traveling to China to proclaim the word of God. They blessed the land with their message of new life in Christ, and also suffered greatly when the darkness clashed with God's light. Their faithful service in spite of great hardship was a beautiful example for Chinese believers to emulate as they served God.

China today still urgently needs more servants and laborers to take the gospel throughout the land. God is looking for people who will stand up and declare, "Lord, here am I. Please send me!"

The day of our Lord is near. May your hearts be encouraged by the testimonies of what the Lord Jesus Christ has done in China, to the praise of his glorious name!

May the Lord raise up more testimonies that would glorify his name in our generation, the next generation, and for evermore!

Lord, you are the victorious king. Blessed are those who follow you to the end!

A humble servant of Christ,
Moses Xie (1918–2011)*

* The late Moses Xie wrote this Preface for the China Chronicles prior to his death in 2011. He was a highly respected Chinese house church leader who spent 23 years of his life in prison for the name of Jesus Christ.

The China Chronicles overview

Many people are aware of the extraordinary explosion of Christianity throughout China in recent decades, with the Church now numbering in excess of 100 million members. Few, however, know how this miracle has occurred. The China Chronicles series is an ambitious project to document the advance of Christianity in each province of China from the time the gospel was first introduced to the present day.

The genesis for this project came at a meeting I attended in the year 2000, where leaders of the Chinese house church movements expressed the need for their members to understand how God established His kingdom throughout China.

As a result, it is planned that these books will be translated into Chinese and distributed widely among the Church, both in China and overseas. Millions of Chinese Christians know little of their spiritual legacy, and my prayer is that multitudes would be strengthened, edified and challenged to carry the torch of the Holy Spirit to their generation.

My intention is not to present readers with a dry list of names and dates but to bring alive the marvelous stories of how God has caused His kingdom to take root and flourish in the world's most populated country.

I consider it a great honor to write these books, especially as I have been entrusted, through hundreds of hours of interviews conducted throughout China, with many testimonies that have never previously been shared in public.

Another reason for compiling the China Chronicles is simply to have a record of God's mighty acts in China.

As a new believer in the 1980s, I recall reading many reports from the Soviet Union of how Christian men and women were being brutally persecuted, yet the kingdom of God grew, with many people meeting Jesus Christ. By the time the Soviet empire collapsed in the early 1990s, no one had systematically recorded the glorious deeds of the Holy Spirit during the Communist era. Tragically, the body of Christ has largely forgotten the miracles God performed in those decades behind the Iron Curtain, and we are much the poorer for it.

Consequently, I am determined to preserve a record of God's mighty acts in China, so that future generations of believers can learn about the wonderful events that have transformed tens of millions of lives there.

At the back of each volume will appear a detailed statistical analysis estimating the number of Christians living in every city and county within each province of China. This is the first comprehensive survey into the number of believers in China—in every one of its more than 2,400 cities and counties—in nearly a century.

Such a huge undertaking would be impossible without the cooperation and assistance of numerous organizations and individuals. I apologize to the many people who helped me in various ways whose names are not mentioned here, many because of security concerns. May the Lord be with you and bless you!

I appreciate the help of mission organizations such as the International Mission Board (IMB), Overseas Missionary Fellowship (OMF), Revival Chinese Ministries International (RCMI) and many others that graciously allowed me access to their archives, libraries, photographs, collections and personal records. I am indebted to the many believers whose generosity exemplifies Jesus' command, "Freely you have received; freely give" (Matthew 10.8).

Many Chinese believers, too numerous to list, have lovingly assisted in this endeavor. For example, I fondly recall the aged house church evangelist Elder Fu, who required two young men to assist him up the stairs to my hotel room because he was eager to be interviewed for this series. Although he had spent many years in prison for the gospel, this saint desperately wanted to testify to God's great works so that believers around the world could be inspired and encouraged to live a more consecrated life. Countless Chinese believers I met and interviewed were similarly keen to share what God has done, to glorify His name.

Finally, I would be remiss not to thank the Lord Jesus Christ. As you read these books, my prayer is that He will emerge from the pages not merely as a historical figure, but as someone ever present, longing to seek and to save the lost by displaying His power and transformative grace.

Today the Church in China is one of the strongest in the world, both spiritually and numerically. Yet little more than a century ago China was considered one of the most difficult mission fields. The great Welsh missionary Griffith John once wrote:

> The good news is moving but very slowly. The people are as hard as steel. They are eaten up both soul and body by the world, and do not seem to feel that there can be reality in anything beyond sense. To them our doctrine is foolishness, our talk jargon. We discuss and beat them in argument. We reason them into silence and shame; but the whole effort falls upon them like showers upon a sandy desert.[1]

How things have changed! When it is all said and done, no person in China will be able to take credit for the amazing revival that has occurred. It will be clear that this great accomplishment is the handiwork of none other than the Lord Jesus Christ. We will stand in awe and declare:

The L ORD has done this,
  and it is marvelous in our eyes.
This is the day the L ORD has made;
  let us rejoice and be glad in it.

(Psalm 118.23–24, NIV 1984)

Paul Hattaway

Publisher's note: In the China Chronicles we have avoided specific information, such as individuals' names or details that could lead directly to the identification of house church workers. The exceptions to this rule are where a leader has already become so well known around the world that there is little point concealing his or her identity in these books. This same principle applies to the use of photographs.

Several different systems for writing the sounds of Chinese characters in English have been used over the years, the main ones being the Wade-Giles system (introduced in 1912) and Pinyin (literally "spelling sounds"), which has been the accepted form in China since 1979. In the China Chronicles, all names of people and places are given in their Pinyin form, although in many instances the old spelling is also given in parentheses. This means that the places formerly spelt Chung-king, Shantung and Tien-tsin are now respectively Chongqing, Shandong and Tianjin; Mao Tse-tung becomes Mao Zedong, and so on. The only times we have retained the old spelling of names is when they are part of the title of a published book or article listed in the Notes or Bibliography.

Introduction

———•—•———

> Guizhou is a land where there are no three days without rain, no
> three fields without a mountain, and no three coins in anyone's
> pocket.
>
> (A Chinese saying)

The Precious Province

The above saying may not be very flattering to the people of
Guizhou, but it is largely true. People who spend any length of
time in the province soon realize it is a rainy, mountainous and
largely impoverished part of China.

The name "Guizhou" itself has interesting origins. For
centuries the area was considered an isolated realm inhabited
by non-Han tribes. People rarely ventured into the region,
which was considered of little consequence to the country as
a whole.

According to Chinese legend, during the Tang Dynasty
(618–907) a tribesman named Pugui emerged from the remote
mountains. He traveled to the Tang capital at Xi'an, where he
begged the emperor to make his region part of the Chinese
empire. When the visitor was asked where he was from, Pugui
replied "Juzhou" in his local minority language, for he was
unable to speak Chinese. "Juzhou" was difficult to pronounce
in the Chinese of the day, so the name Guizhou was given to
the region instead. It has been known as Guizhou ever since.

The Chinese character for *gui* has several meanings. Today
it denotes something that is highly valued, precious, expensive
or worthy. In ancient Chinese, however, the original character

Guizhou's Hongguoshu waterfall is the largest in China
IMB

used for *gui* meant "demon" or "devil," thus the territory was known as "the land of demons."

Guizhou, which is home to 35 million people today, is located in the rugged mountains of southwest China. Its inhabitants come from more than 80 distinct ethnic groups, each speaking its own language, although the government refuses to recognize most of these groups. For the purpose of administrative ease, it has combined many unique tribes and people groups together under the banner of one of China's officially recognized "minority nationalities."

With an area of just over 68,000 square miles (176,000 sq. km), Guizhou is approximately the same size as the US states of

Missouri and Oklahoma, but it contains six times as many people as Missouri and its population is nine times larger than Oklahoma.

By another comparison, Guizhou covers an area larger than England, Wales and Northern Ireland combined, but contains only about 60 percent as many people as those three countries of the United Kingdom.

No three days without rain

Guizhou is known for its somewhat depressing weather. The mountains that protect the province from the rest of China also influence its weather patterns. As a result, much of Guizhou is enshrined by mist-covered mountains, and rain often settles in for weeks at a time. Reflecting this reality, the name of the provincial capital, Guiyang, means "Precious Sun."

Despite its abundant rainfall, Guizhou has also experienced severe droughts and famines over the course of its history. Most of the province has rocky and poor soil, which hampers food production. A severe drought afflicted Guizhou as recently as 2010, causing the government to step in and provide relief.

Due to the grinding poverty and frequent hardships of life in Guizhou, in recent decades many people have fled the province for more desirable parts of China. Indeed, between 2000 and 2010, the population of Guizhou fell by half a million people. Most of the exodus occurred from rural farming areas, with some counties recording drops of more than 20 percent of their population during the decade. The mass migrations have caused large problems in society. As masses of young people grow up without their parents, thousands have become homeless and have turned to crime to survive. A report in 2017 highlighted some of the consequences of this social dislocation:

> In June last year, four left-behind children from the same family, ranging from ages five to 13, committed suicide together

by swallowing pesticide in Bijie, in impoverished Guizhou province . . . In November 2012, five boys died from carbon monoxide poisoning after starting a charcoal fire trying to stay warm inside a dumpster. The problem of left-behind children is most severe in . . . the key sources of migrant workers, where 44 per cent of rural children live without their mother or father.[1]

The national government's solution to the problem of poverty in Guizhou has been to bulldoze entire villages in many areas, and to relocate people to government-subsidized apartments, often against the will of the families that have lived in their locations for generations.[2] In 2016, a total of 750,000 poor people in Guizhou were relocated to 3,600 newly constructed locations.

No three fields without a mountain

When Mao Zedong launched his campaign to modernize China by constructing new roads, train lines and airports, Guizhou presented great challenges due to its rough terrain and millions of tribal inhabitants with little or no knowledge of Chinese language or culture.

In the late 1970s, the government finally managed to construct a road through one county in southern Guizhou. To celebrate the achievement, a group of officials decided to visit a village that was now linked to the outside world for the first time. Climbing into a fleet of four-wheel-drive vehicles, the officials endured many hours of back-breaking travel on the freshly created roadway, their wheels just inches from the edge of cliffs, with sheer drops of thousands of feet to the valley floor below.

When they finally arrived at their destination, the officials tried to book the best room in the village, only to discover there was no accommodation, and few of the minority people could speak Chinese. After finally finding someone they could communicate with, the officials were invited to stay in the home of the village leader.

As a meal was prepared for the esteemed guests, the locals gathered around the vehicles, with confused and bewildered looks on their faces. Their culture required them to show hospitality to strangers, but they had never before seen anyone like these visitors.

In a bid to display kindness, the women of the village collected handfuls of straw, which they stuffed into the radiator grilles of the jeeps. They had never seen a motorized vehicle before, and in their innocence had assumed the jeeps were a species of large animal they had not previously encountered!

Although most of Guizhou has been dragged into the current century since then, approximately half of the villages in the province remain without electricity and are unconnected by road.

Mountains make up 87 percent of Guizhou's topography, and most of its population lives at an average altitude of 3,280 feet (1,000 meters) above sea level. Many parts of the province remain unexplored, with some areas in the north and west described as China's "wild west."

The Liupanshui region in western Guizhou has a particularly bad reputation, with many Chinese refusing to travel there. Parts of the prefecture are so remote and undeveloped that even today, gangs of bandits occasionally raid the towns before escaping on horseback into the inhospitable mountains.

No three coins in anyone's pocket

These days—especially since Beijing hosted the 2008 Olympics—China is viewed around the world as a modern country, with impressive skyscrapers and extraordinary infrastructure. Many tourists who have visited China's main centers would struggle to believe just how backward parts of Guizhou are. Millions of people live hidden among remote mountain peaks and valleys, away from the main transportation arteries. In those places there are few roads, and the inhabitants continue to experience dire poverty.

Guizhou is indisputably one of the poorest regions of China. It officially ranks 26th out of 31 provinces for gross domestic product (GDP), and for centuries families have struggled to eke out a living in the inhospitable mountains. For much of the nineteenth century, the major export from Guizhou was opium, as people tried to derive an income any way they could.

Today, Guizhou's wealth is concentrated in Guiyang and other urban centers, and only some resources and jobs have trickled down to the countryside. Countless villages are still trapped in excruciating poverty, and between 60 and 70 percent of the population in rural areas remains illiterate.

When the Communists passed through Guizhou in 1934 on their famous Long March, the soldiers were horrified by the condition of the Miao people. One shocked reporter noted:

> They sat huddled in nakedness beside straw cooking fires . . . Girls of 17 and 18 worked naked in the fields. Many families had only one pair of trousers to share among three or four adult males . . . They owned no land. They were in debt to the landlord from birth to death. There was no escape. They sold their children if anyone would buy them. They smothered or drowned baby girls. That was routine. The boys were killed too, if there was no market for them.[3]

Guizhou has the highest fertility rate of any province in China, and families with eight or nine children are not uncommon in rural areas. Because of the gender imbalance caused by China's one-child policy, in recent years many girls in Guizhou have been sold to human traffickers from other parts of the country, who in turn sell the girls as wives or sex slaves to the highest bidder. Tragically, many of the girls taken away into this life of despair are not kidnapped, but have been willingly sold by their desperate families. Some girls have been sold for as little as 200 Yuan (about $29).

Marco Polo in the province of Ciuju

In the 1270s, after the intrepid Venetian explorer Marco Polo became the first European to visit today's Yunnan Province, he ventured eastward into the "Province of Ciuju," which most scholars believe to be areas in today's western Guizhou. After traveling for 12 days, Polo described coming "to a great and noble city which is called Fungul."[4] Although historians remain baffled as to the modern-day identity of the city, the explorer provided a compelling picture of life there:

> The people are idolaters and subject to the Great Kaan, and live by trade and handicrafts. You must know they manufacture stuffs of the bark of certain trees which form very fine summer clothing. They are good soldiers, and have paper-money. For you must understand that henceforward we are in the countries where the Great Kaan's paper-money is current.[5]

As he continued his journey northward toward Sichuan Province, Marco Polo detailed the scourge that "lions" had inflicted on the people of the region. Without doubt, he was describing the abundance of tigers that continued to ravage communities in western Guizhou until the mid-twentieth century. Polo remarked:

> The country swarms with [tigers] to that degree that no man can venture to sleep outside his house at night. Moreover, when you travel on the river, and come to a halt at night, unless you keep a good way from the bank the [tigers] will spring on the

boat and snatch one of the crew and make off with him and devour him. And but for a certain help that the inhabitants enjoy, no one could venture to travel in that province, because of the multitude of those [tigers], and because of their strength and ferocity.[6]

The peoples of Guizhou

Guizhou is one of China's most ethnically diverse provinces, although 62 percent of the population are Han Chinese, most of whom speak the Southwest dialect of Mandarin. The largest of the officially recognized minority groups in the province are the Miao (4.3 million), Bouyei (2.8 million), Dong (1.6 million) and Tujia (1.4 million).

The Horned Miao—one of more than 80 ethnic groups in Guizhou—are so named because women customarily wear wooden horns affixed to their hair
Robert Sussland

The numerous other minority groups in Guizhou include the Yi (843,000), Gelao (559,000), Shui (370,000) and Yao (45,000), in addition to several smaller tribes that the government has lumped together into a list of "Undetermined Minorities."[7]

Altogether, the vibrant and colorful ethnic groups provide much of the character and culture of Guizhou, and without them life would be much more drab and uninspiring. Each year the minority people throughout the province celebrate nearly a thousand festivals, which provide a boost to the economy and help each group to preserve its fascinating customs, dress and handicrafts.

The province is also home to much attractive scenery. Tourists flock to China's largest waterfall—the impressive Hongguoshu Falls—while not far away, Ziyun County boasts the largest cave in the world, at an elevation of 6,000 feet (1,800 meters) above sea level. The Miao Room Cavern was declared the world's largest cave in 2014 and could fit approximately 22 football fields in its interior. When researchers for *National Geographic* officially measured the cave, they found more than a hundred people living inside it, and the cave even contained a school with a basketball court and other facilities. The Chinese government appeared embarrassed by the publicity the cave attracted, and has since closed the school and evicted the residents, declaring, "China is not a society of cavemen."

A land of slaughter

For much of its history, Guizhou has been the staging ground for numerous wars, with the Chinese struggling for centuries to subdue the "barbarian tribes" in the province.

Prior to the 1500s, Guizhou was inhabited almost entirely by ethnic minorities, with the Miao being the dominant group. As waves of Han settlers migrated into the province over the next

300 years, the Miao and other peoples were marginalized and pushed off the best land by the more sophisticated and better-equipped Han.

As the Miao were forced deeper into the inhospitable mountains, they resisted their oppressors and frequent clashes erupted. Han settlers often responded by calling on the support of the government, and troops were dispatched to quell what they considered "barbarian uprisings." In reality, most Miao were kind and peace-loving people, but they had been backed into a corner. The mountains of Guizhou became the scene for numerous genocide campaigns designed to wipe out the Miao.

During the latter part of the Ming Dynasty (1368–1644), more than 80 military campaigns were launched against the Miao. The Imperial Court even attempted to isolate the Miao territory from the rest of China by erecting walls to keep the Miao confined to the mountains. In 1650 the Miao rebelled, tore down the walls, and "demolished the border between themselves and the Chinese."[8]

The conflict continued, with the Chinese attempting to batter the Miao into submission. In 1726, when the Qing rulers sent garrisons to crush another Miao uprising, Chinese soldiers reportedly:

> set more than 1,000 Miao villages on fire, butchered tens of thousands of people, and destroyed their farmland. In response, in 1727 various Miao tribes unified against the Chinese, constructing stone signal towers at one-mile intervals along mountain ridges. The Miao took blood oaths to fight the Chinese to the death. They even killed their own wives and children, so they could face the advancing enemy as men with nothing to lose.[9]

Among the extensive annals of brutality waged by the Chinese against the Miao, perhaps the most vicious campaign commenced in 1800. A vast army was mobilized from across China in a bid to exterminate the Miao completely. At the time, critics describing the scale of the war said that "elephant guns were used to hunt rabbits."

The Miao survived this and many other onslaughts, aided by their matchless knowledge of the mountains in Guizhou. They became so adept at fighting that the Chinese required 18 years (1855–72) to quell one rebellion. Consequently, when a British traveler visited Guizhou in 1874 he reported:

> Every village I passed through showed sad signs of the savage havoc made by the raids of the Miao . . . This province of Guizhou is sadly devastated, and all the cities are reduced to mere villages, and the villages to a mere collection of straw huts. Everywhere ruins of good substantial houses abound, and show what a prosperous region this once was before the wild men of the hills came down *en masse* and butchered the whole population. This occurred 20 years ago and still the devoted cities remain as cities of the dead, with extensive walls surrounding acres of ruin.[10]

The grim legacy of war

After centuries of genocide and conflict in Guizhou, many scars remained just beneath the surface of people's lives. The efforts to obliterate the Miao from the face of the earth led to many of their communities becoming extremely insular. Understandably, they viewed the Han as their enemies, and they shunned outsiders in general, including Miao people from other subgroups.

Despite their tragic past, the Miao have managed to retain their reputation as a friendly people. They offer warm hospitality to visitors and strangers, even when they don't have much themselves. Their generosity has remained constant despite the centuries of war, suffering and slavery they endured at the hands of outsiders.

Evidence of the centuries of Chinese military campaigns can be seen in the composition of Guizhou's population today, with several distinct Chinese people groups inhabiting the province. They are the descendants of soldiers who were sent to quell Miao uprisings centuries ago. The two largest groups are the 350,000 Chuanlan ("blue clad") people, and the 800,000 Chuanqing ("black clad") people. Both groups, so named because of the predominant color of their clothing, inhabit areas near the provincial capital Guiyang.

Other similar Chinese groups in Guizhou include the 120,000 Nanjingren ("Nanjing people") who are descended from troops sent to the area from Nanjing in east China, and a small group of 4,000 Shenzhou people who settled in Guizhou after a military campaign centuries ago. These groups now view themselves as minority people, and they retain distinct dress and customs to the present day.

Finally, according to one historian, Guizhou also used to be "the dumping ground for hardcore criminals who had committed heinous crimes in central China. Sent there as exiles, they lived hard lives filled with hate. Their descendants inherited these harsh lives from their forefathers."[11]

Altogether, this rough collection of tribes and migrants have combined to form a vibrant patchwork of people in China's Precious Province.

A word on Guizhou's ethnic composition

Many outsiders may struggle to appreciate the level of ethnic and cultural diversity in Guizhou, unless they visit the province and experience it for themselves. The Chinese government, however, does not officially recognize most of the distinct peoples of Guizhou. In the 1950s they combined various tribes together under broad categories for purposes of administrative ease. For example, they created the large and generic Miao nationality and squeezed dozens of distinct tribes into it. They did similar things with the Yi, Yao and other official classifications.

As a result of this policy, today many distinct people groups in Guizhou tend "not to exist." In some cases, tribes have been combined with groups they have been at enmity with for centuries. Some groups don't understand a word of each other's language, possess different histories and customs, and may even forbid marriage between members of their tribe and the nationality that the government now tells them they are part of.

Why Christians should care

The government's refusal to accept the unique differences of the people groups in Guizhou should be no excuse for the Christian world to follow suit.

Each tribe and ethnic group, regardless of size, is precious in God's sight. He created their unique and colorful cultures to display His creative glory. The Bible teaches that the matchless plan of God's salvation through Jesus Christ will one day reach its fulfillment in heaven, when four living creatures and 24 elders will sing a new song:

> You are worthy to take the scroll
>   and to open its seals,
> because you were slain,
>   and with your blood you purchased for God
>   persons from *every tribe and language and people and
>   nation.*
> You have made them to be a kingdom and priests to serve
>   our God,
>   and they will reign on the earth.
>   (Revelation 5.9–10, emphasis added)

13

Unfortunately, many mission organizations and Chinese Christians today appear unable to grasp the importance of viewing the ethnic diversity of Guizhou's peoples as they really are. Most Christians have followed the government's classifications, finding it more convenient to work with fewer than 20 official "minority nationalities" in Guizhou than to reach more than 80 distinct groups.

This lack of understanding has led to many people groups being passed over by the gospel. For example, many Christians are aware of the extraordinary people movement to God among the A-Hmao in the early twentieth century. Today, approximately 80 percent of the people in this tribe continue to follow Jesus Christ. Instead of being recognized as a distinct people, however, the A-Hmao were put into the government-constructed Miao nationality, along with more than 30 other tribes throughout Guizhou, most of which speak mutually unintelligible languages.

Many mission organizations assume that if God reached one "Miao" group then surely they can reach the others without much difficulty. The reality has proved sharply different, however. The A-Hmao Christians found they needed to engage in difficult cross-cultural evangelism in order to bridge the barriers that exist between them and other Miao groups.

The importance of names

In this book I have decided to use, as much as possible, the names that people groups use for themselves, and to avoid the labels that both the Chinese and missionaries traditionally applied to them. The above-mentioned A-Hmao tribespeople, for example, were commonly called Da Hua ("Big Flowery") Miao by outsiders, because of the designs on the women's traditional capes, and also to distinguish them from the less populous Gha-Mu tribe (labeled the "Small Flowery" Miao). Neither group, in its own language, calls itself Miao at all, as "Miao" is a Chinese word.

Some groups in Guizhou reject the Chinese labels assigned to their tribes and consider the names derogatory. In this book, therefore, I have generally used the autonyms that tribes use for themselves.

I have been privileged to travel extensively throughout Guizhou Province since the late 1980s. When I began to use the names that the ethnic groups of Guizhou call themselves, I often saw the people's faces light up in amazement and appreciation that an outsider cared enough to learn the true name of their people. This simple step is an excellent starting point for any preachers of the gospel who hope to reach the precious peoples of Guizhou. Regrettably, most Christians continue to use the government designations, and a gilt-edged opportunity to understand and share the gospel with dozens of unique tribes is going to waste.

God's broken heart

For centuries, the almighty God has looked down from heaven upon the people of Guizhou, desiring to know them as His children. He witnessed the massacres and genocide of generations of Miao, while patiently awaiting the arrival of the first messengers of the gospel who would take the good news of Jesus to them.

In the first volume of this series of books, many remarkable stories of revival revealed how the Church in Shandong Province blossomed under the mighty hand of God. The history of Christianity in Guizhou is notably different, and has been marked with intense struggle and difficulties. The churches have battled numerous obstacles, yet as the following pages will reveal, the living God has brought His salvation to Guizhou through a series of remarkable events that totally transformed several people groups and entire communities.

In this book, the stories of Christian efforts to reach several of Guizhou's largest ethnicities have warranted their own chapters, which are scattered throughout. One group that has not been given its own section, however, is the A-Hmao. The remarkable Christian history among the A-Hmao has dominated the narrative of missionary work in the province, and those accounts have been chronologically dispersed throughout the book in the chapters that examine each decade.

Today, approximately 2.7 million people in Guizhou identify themselves as Christians, a number that has grown exponentially from just 100,000 professing believers at the advent of Communism in 1949.[12]

My hope and prayer is that you will be encouraged, inspired and challenged as you read about how the Holy Spirit transformed entire communities in Guizhou. May you too be brought to your knees and experience personal spiritual revival.

The mysterious origins of the Miao

When snow covered the ground

Any visit to Guizhou Province is incomplete without a trip to a Miao festival. The Miao, who number approximately five million people in Guizhou alone, have millions more in other areas of south China and throughout the mountains of Southeast Asia, where they are better known by the name of their dominant subgroup, the Hmong.

In 1924, F. M. Savina of the Paris Foreign Missionary Society published a book in which he claimed the Miao were of Caucasian origin. Savina wrote, "In appearance the Miao are pale yellow in complexion, almost white, their hair is often

The possible Caucasian origin of the Miao people can be seen in the fair complexion of this young girl in Guizhou
Miao Messenger

light or dark brown, sometimes even red or corn-silk blond, and a few even have pale blue eyes."[1]

For many centuries the Chinese living in the Miao regions called themselves the Li-min, which is generally translated "black-haired people." One historian has asked, "Why, then, did they designate themselves the Black or Dark people? Did they at one time live in the neighborhood of people who were fair-haired and of lighter complexion than themselves?"[2]

During intense periods of Chinese persecution, many Miao were killed because they were easy to single out. An 80-year-old Miao man in Laos, Cher Sue Vue, remembered his childhood when the Chinese crossed into Laos searching for white babies. He said, "At that time there was only one white baby in our village. The infant's parents were warned before the Chinese arrived, and they carried him into the forest where they hid."[3]

Speculation about the origins of the Miao has led some to claim that the ancestors of the Miao first lived in Persia or Babylon before migrating into Siberia. After staying there for a time, the Miao moved again, passing through Mongolia and entering north China.

Chinese histories confirm that the Miao once lived in north and central China before they were pushed south. For centuries the Miao have passed down oral histories from one generation to the next. One of their legends tells of a homeland where "days and nights lasted six months, the water was frozen, and snow hid the ground. Only a few trees grew and they were small. The people, too, were short and squat, clothed in furs."[4]

Genesis according to the Miao

The mysterious origins of the Miao are made even more intriguing by their oral traditions, handed down in song and in couplets, where each alternate sentence acts as a definition of

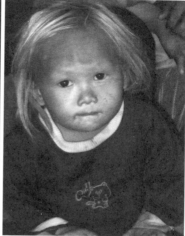

Two young Miao girls with blond hair
Miao Messenger

the first. This method has helped their stories and genealogies to be remembered with great accuracy. At funerals and weddings among some Miao groups today, the ancestry of the bride and groom are recited all the way back to Adam.

From their genealogies, it can be seen that some Miao tribes trace their ancestry back to Japheth and Gomer, which some scholars argue would make them of Indo-European stock. If this theory holds true, it would support the speculation that the Miao originated in today's Middle East or Central Asia.

While it's impossible to prove or disprove these theories, Miao wedding and funeral recitations have helped the Christian message enter into the hearts of many Miao people over the past century.[5]

Early anthropologists were astounded when they first recorded Miao creation legends among communities that had been driven out of Jiangxi Province. One account closely mirrored the biblical record of creation, the fall of humankind, and other key events from the book of Genesis. This convinced some scholars that the Miao have managed to preserve the story of their origins with remarkable accuracy over thousands of years, although the account of the flood varies from tribe to tribe.

Some of the more interesting parts of the ancient Miao creation story are included here, as translated by Edgar Truax of the Institute for Creation Research:[6]

"The Creation"
On the day God created the heavens and earth.
On that day He opened the gateway of light.
In the earth then He made heaps of earth and of stone.
In the sky He made bodies, the sun and the moon.
In the earth He created the hawk and the kite.
In the water created the lobster and fish.
In the wilderness made He the tiger and bear,
Made verdure to cover the mountains,
Made forest extend with the ranges,
Made the light green cane,
Made the rank bamboo.

"Man"
On the earth He created a man from the dirt.
Of the man thus created, a woman He formed . . .
So the earth began filling with tribes and with families.
Creation was shared by the clans and the peoples.

"The World Wicked"
These did not God's will nor returned His affection . . .
Their leaders shook fists in the face of the Mighty
Then the earth was convulsed to the depth of three strata.
Rending the air to the uttermost heaven.
God's anger arose till His Being was changed;
His wrath flaring up filled His eyes and His face.
Until He must come and demolish humanity.
Come and destroy a whole world full of people.

"The Flood"
So it poured forty days in sheets and in torrents.
Then fifty-five days of misting and drizzle.
The waters surmounted the mountains and ranges.
The deluge ascending leapt valley and hollow.
An earth with no earth upon which to take refuge!
A world with no foothold where one might subsist!
The people were baffled, impotent and ruined,
Despairing, horror stricken, diminished and finished.
But the Patriarch Nuah was righteous.
The Matriarch Gaw Bo-lu-en upright.
Built a boat very wide.
Made a ship very vast.
Their household entire got aboard and were floated,
The family complete rode the deluge in safety.
The animals with him were female and male.
The birds went along and were mated in pairs . . .

"Babel"
Their descendants established encampments and cities.
Their singing was all with the same tunes and music;
Their speaking was all with the same words and language.
Then they said let us build us a very big city;
Let us raise unto heaven a very high tower.
This was wrong, but they reached this decision;
Not right, but they rashly persisted.
God struck at them then, changed their language and
    accent.
Descending in wrath, He confused tones and voices.
One's speech to the others who hear him has no meaning;
He's speaking in words, but they can't understand him.
So the city they built was never completed;
The tower they wrought has to stand thus unfinished.
In despair then they separate under all heaven,
They part from each other the globe to encircle.
They arrive at six corners and speak the six languages.

Early Christian martyrs

Waves of persecution

Although the earliest Christian presence in China dates back to the Tang Dynasty (618–907), no evidence exists of Christian influence of any kind in Guizhou until 1765, when the first Catholic missionaries arrived in the province.

The Vatican handed responsibility for Guizhou to the Paris Foreign Missionary Society. A succession of Frenchmen soon began to arrive, and by 1771 they counted 210 converts throughout the province.[1]

Many of the French missionaries and their Chinese converts suffered terrible persecution as they sought to establish churches in Guizhou. Waves of brutality hammered the fledgling believers, but they stood firm and rejoiced at having been found worthy to suffer for the name of Jesus Christ.

One of the first followers of Christ to be martyred for the faith in Guizhou was Wu Guosheng, who was widely known as a violent man before he met Jesus. The transformation in his character was so stark that after surrendering his life to God he led 128 of his relatives and friends to the faith. Wu reportedly:

> resolved to be a true disciple of Christ and to do whatever was necessary to see God's kingdom established in his home area, even if it meant hardship and persecution to himself. Through the power of prayer and his bold witness the number of believers in Longping grew to more than 600 by 1811 . . .

Just when a major breakthrough seemed imminent in 1814, a widespread persecution broke out. On April 3 of that year Wu

Wu Guosheng
CRBC

was imprisoned and tortured in an attempt to break his spirit and cause him to denounce Christ, but he endured the cruel punishments and remained firm in his faith. Wu wrote a letter to his anguished wife from prison, exhorting her to "Be loyal to the Lord and accept His will."

In prison, Wu was a great example to the other inmates. He was full of the joy of the Lord and constantly led them in songs of praise . . . His last words before being executed on November 7, 1814, were "Heaven, heaven, my true home!"[2]

One of Wu Guosheng's colleagues, a 61-year-old man named Zhang Dapeng, was executed for his faith the following year. Zhang grew up in a non-Christian home in Duyun without any knowledge of the gospel. As a young man he moved to Guiyang, where he went into the lucrative silk business.

Sometime later, Zhang heard the gospel and placed his faith in Jesus Christ. He was not allowed to receive baptism, however, because at the time of his conversion he kept a concubine, which was a standard practice for wealthy Chinese men of the era. In 1797 a preacher pointed out that the eternal

Zhang Dapeng
CRBC

ramifications of living in such a sinful union far outweighed the temporal benefits. Zhang was convicted of his sin, and he left his concubine and was baptized.

After hearing of the baptism, Zhang's two younger brothers strongly opposed him, enraged that his association with Christianity had tarnished their family's good name. Undeterred, Zhang felt he had wasted the first part of his life and thus became a zealous evangelist, sharing the good news with as many people as possible. He even purchased a house on a busy city street so that he could reach more unbelievers.

More than 200 Chinese Christians were arrested and tortured during a major crackdown in 1815. Zhang went into hiding but was betrayed by his brother-in-law. In prison Zhang shared the gospel with his cellmates, and was offered freedom after his family members begged for clemency. The prison authorities agreed he could gain his release on one condition—he must first renounce his faith in Christ. Zhang Dapeng refused and was executed on February 2, 1815.

Liu Wenyuan
CRBC

A few decades later, Liu Wenyuan was added to the roll of martyrs for Jesus Christ in Guizhou. Born into a simple farming family in 1760, Liu grew up helping his family grow vegetables, and he later inherited the farm.

When Liu was 37, a Christian passed through his village and told him about the way of salvation. Liu was so convicted by the Holy Spirit that he immediately went to Guiyang, the provincial capital, to learn more about the faith. His soul was like a dry sponge, soaking in every drop of information. Liu repented of his sins and put his faith in Christ, and he began to share the gospel with everyone he met.

Extreme hardship was not far away for Liu Wenyuan. In 1800 he was arrested with five other believers and exiled to northeast China, "where he was sold as a slave and for 30 years was treated worse than a dog by [the family that owned him]. He suffered all torture and humiliation, making no complaint but rather offering it all to God."[3]

In 1830 a general pardon was declared for all exiled prisoners throughout China. Now aged 70, Liu made the long journey home, only to find that after 30 years' absence, all recollection of him had long since faded. Liu was kept from utter despair, however, by the comfort of the Holy Spirit and the promise that the Lord Jesus would never leave nor forsake his children. Finally, after much effort, he was able to locate his wife and his two sons who were now grown adults.

Liu returned to growing vegetables to earn a living, but four years later the authorities launched another severe persecution against Christians. This time the 74-year-old Liu was ignored, but his sons and a daughter-in-law were arrested. Having been separated from his family for so much of his life, Liu Wenyuan:

> disguised himself and succeeded in meeting his sons, whom he encouraged to be steadfast in the faith. However, a soldier recognized him as a Christian, immediately jailed him and put him to the severest torture. He was not discouraged, but prayed constantly and sang praises to God.[4]

Despite again being threatened with exile, Liu refused to renounce his Savior. The authorities, maddened by his stubborn faith, dispatched Liu's second son and daughter-in-law to northwest China. A few months later his eldest son died in prison. Through his grief, Liu was nevertheless overjoyed that his sons had persevered for Christ.

Meanwhile, back in Guizhou, Liu Wenyuan was in prayer one day when a white cloth appeared before him in a vision. When he reached out to pick it up, the cloth disappeared. Liu took it as a sign that he would soon die, for in China white cloth is associated with death and mourning. A short time later, on May 17, 1834, the provincial authorities in Guiyang ordered his arrest and execution. When the death sentence was carried out, astonished eyewitnesses reported:

> A ball of fire came down from heaven and rested over his head, and an angel appeared to wipe the blood from his face. The

angel carried his soul to heaven and the next day his wife came to carry his body away for burial in his own vegetable garden.[5]

Five years of fury

A period of relative calm came upon believers in Guizhou, with few martyrdoms for Christ during the next couple of decades. The peace abruptly ended in 1857, however, when a fierce and sustained persecution broke out. By 1862, when the storm subsided, many believers had been put to death, and Christians were left in disarray throughout the province.

Lu Tingmei, Wang Bin and Agatha Lin Zhao
CRBC

In 1857, three believers were killed at Guiyang. One of them was Lu Tingmei, a respected Christian from the Bouyei minority group. By the time he was 38, Lu was a wealthy man with a wife, two sons and a daughter. He joined a Buddhist sect, but it failed to satisfy his inner longing for peace and joy. When he read some Christian books, however, the words had a profound effect on his heart and mind. He renounced his involvement with the sect and decided that Jesus Christ was the truth. From that time on, Lu was a zealous disciple, and he brought his father, sister and some friends to the faith.

Lu Tingmei's zeal for the Lord incensed many, and in 1854 he was falsely accused of treason. He was horribly tortured in prison before finally, on December 14, 1857, he was led to the execution ground along with fellow believers Wang Bing and Agatha Lin Zhao.

Wang Bing was a gifted evangelist. In 1854 he was sent to Pingyue and Weng'an to preach the gospel, and many people came to Christ. The following year he visited Pu'an, where the same thing occurred. Wherever Wang went throughout Guizhou he left behind new converts and strengthened the faith of believers.

Agatha Lin Zhao came from Guizhou's Qinglong County. Even before her birth, Lin's family had suffered for the Lord Jesus Christ, with her father imprisoned for the faith.

When Lin was arrested and appeared before a magistrate, the wicked man mocked her vow of chastity and insinuated that no woman of such beauty could possibly have remained a virgin. This disgraceful slander angered Wang Bing and Lu Tingmei. They spoke up in defense of the 40-year-old Lin Zhao, and in a furious rage the magistrate "condemned all three to death and they were executed the following day. After death, stripped of her clothes, she was discovered to be indeed a virgin, and the magistrate admitted his mistake."[6]

Two years later, in July 1861, local officials persecuted the faculty and students at a Bible school in Yaojiaguan. One of the teachers, Luo Tingyin, was captured and dragged off to the city.

Luo had been saved after he heard a street preacher share the gospel. He was transfixed; the words seemed to burn into his heart and soul, and he became a Christian and was baptized soon after. One account of his life says, "His zeal brought not only his wife, but also his parents and the whole household to believe in God. Then, continuing to rely on God's grace, he was able to bring many people to the faith."[7]

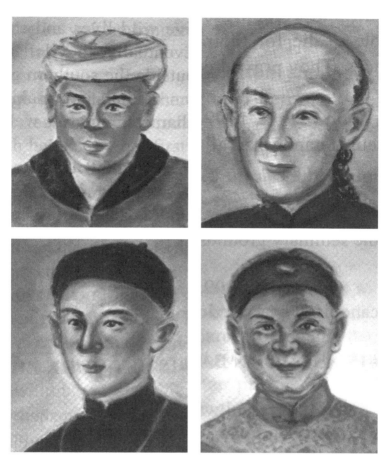

Luo Tingyin, Zhang Wenlan, Chen Changping and Martha Wang-Luo Mande
CRBC

As the 36-year-old Luo Tingyin was being hauled off to Guiyang for trial, the soldiers met up with students Zhang Wenlan and Chen Changping, who were returning after buying provisions for the school. The soldiers bound the trio and took them to an abandoned temple, where they entertained themselves by torturing their helpless victims for days. Luo's wife came and pleaded with him to return home and take care of her and their children. Knowing that the only way to gain his freedom was to deny Christ, Luo "insisted on her remaining firm in her commitment to the Lord and to care for their two sons."[8]

On July 29, 1861, the emperor sent a decree ordering the release of the three Christians. The magistrate was not happy and purposely delayed the publication of the decree so that he could put Luo, Zhang and Chen to death.

Meanwhile, a 59-year-old cook at the Bible school, Martha Wang-Luo Mande, decided to serve the imprisoned men by bringing them food and washing their clothes. The captors mocked and ridiculed Martha for her servitude, but she refused to be intimidated, believing that by serving her brethren she was serving Christ. On the day that the three men were executed, Martha was washing their clothes at the riverbank. One account says:

> When they were being led to the execution ground, she followed along in spite of the soldiers' threats: "I will cut your head off!" Not to be scared off, she answered, "If they can die, so can I" . . . All four showed such courage, being able to die for their faith, that people saw only peace and joy on their faces. They prayed up to the very moment they were beheaded.[9]

Five martyrs in Kaiyang

In February 1862, another group of Christians was put to death in Guizhou. This time a 30-year-old French missionary, Jean-Pierre Néel, was numbered among the five who were slain in Kaiyang.

Néel was arrested with four Chinese believers (Chen Xianheng, Wu Xueshang, Zhang Yianshen and Lucy Yi Zhenmei) when a mob of a hundred men, some on horseback,

Jean-Pierre Néel

descended on the place they were staying. The mob "tied the French missionary's pigtail to the tail of the horse. He was made to walk or run according to the whim of the horseman, to the great joy of the troops."[10]

Before the executions were carried out, soldiers were permitted to abuse and torture the prisoners at their pleasure, but all efforts to make them renounce Christ were firmly rejected. They were not tempted to trade in the treasures of Christ for momentary relief.

The execution date was set for February 18, 1862. In the morning, the five faithful believers were bound and led through Kaiyang, where people lined the streets to jeer and mock them. Taking the humiliation with joy, the Christians asked God for strength. They were beheaded, starting with Jean-Pierre Néel. Eyewitnesses testified that immediately after he died:

> A beam of light appeared in the sky. The officials and all the non-Christians saw it and were surprised. The persecutors hung

the heads of the five martyrs on the town gate as a warning to the people against faith in the Christian religion, but some believers by night secretly removed them and put them in one coffin, which they then buried in an old tomb.[11]

Such was the sustained ferocity of opposition in Guizhou that by 1886, more than 120 years after first arriving, the Catholic churches contained a total of just 5,000 members throughout the entire province.[12] By that time they had been joined in Guizhou by the first Evangelical missionaries.

1870s and 1880s

The first Evangelicals

Guizhou was one of the last provinces in China to open up to Evangelical Christianity. The call for workers was first made by the great missionary Hudson Taylor, who strongly advocated for the province. In one of the first magazines published by the China Inland Mission (CIM) in 1875, Taylor gave this overview of Guizhou:

> The capital, near the center of the province, is the smallest provincial capital of the 18, the walls being only two miles round. The other chief towns are all of inferior note . . . "Miao" is used by the Chinese as a general term for all the dwellers of these mountains, but is not applied to every tribe by the people themselves. They consist of over 41 tribes in all . . . They have little or no knowledge of the One true and living God even as revealed in nature, and they know nothing of Him as revealed in His Word, and in the person and work of the Lord Jesus Christ.[1]

Eighteen months after Taylor's article, the honor of being the first Evangelical missionaries to set foot in Guizhou went to Englishmen Charles Judd and his brother-in-law James Broumton, who traveled together through Hunan Province before reaching Guiyang in 1877. Their journey was a perilous one, with the duo nearly perishing by both water and fire before reaching their destination. Judd recalled, "Our boat stuck severely on a rock and sprung a leak, which had we not at once discovered, would soon have let us down into the deep water."[2]

James Broumton and Charles Judd—the first Evangelical missionaries in Guizhou

Days later, the pioneers had to scramble down a burning mountainside. To escape the fire, they ran into a thicket of thorns and cutgrass, which tore Judd's hands open. Broumton, meanwhile, had become separated and was close to being engulfed by the intense flames surrounding him on every side. He wrote:

The fire was fast gaining on us. Nothing but a change of wind was likely to save us. We looked to Him who alone rules the wind, and for a few moments it turned in the opposite direction. The fire was stayed, and we rushed by, feeling its burning heat as we passed. It was some little time before we could breathe freely, as we felt the narrowness of our escape. The Lord had preserved us.[3]

At Huangping, Judd and Broumton encountered the Miao people for the first time. Judd remarked:

> We were strongly impressed with the simple open-hearted character of these people. May the Lord of the harvest speedily send some of His laborers to work in that part of His vineyard. Should any brother missionary be inclined to make them the special objects of his labor of faith and love, I think that Guiyang would be an excellent place to commence from.[4]

Upon finally reaching Guizhou's capital, the duo reported:

> We preached several times to crowds on the streets, who bought our books and tracts with avidity. I do not remember once having the least incivility shown to us in the city, and scarcely anywhere in the whole province. Nowhere in China have I traveled with such ease, and the goodwill of the people. We had many opportunities to tell of the Savior's grace.[5]

After helping his brother-in-law rent a house in Guiyang, Judd returned to Hunan, while Broumton soon found favor with the local officials in the capital. On his first Easter in the city, he decided to visit a local Catholic church, where he was astounded to find 1,600 communicants. The Catholics had already been deeply embedded in the province for more than a century, and Broumton felt it would take much effort and time to convince them "of the errors of the Church to which they belong."

In early 1878, after renting a building to use as a chapel, Broumton wrote:

> This chapel . . . will seat 50 or 60 persons. God grant that many souls would be born-again through the Word that shall be proclaimed in this humble little room . . . Oh, how I long for more acquaintance with the language, so as to tell them more plainly of the grace of God that brings salvation . . . Many of the people know something of the gospel, as there are a great

number of Romanists. At least they know that there is one God, and a Savior Jesus Christ. God grant they may soon have a saving knowledge of the living God, and of Jesus Christ whom He has sent.[6]

As the 1870s drew to a close, several Evangelical missionaries in other parts of China moved to Guizhou, encouraged by Broumton's success in gaining a foothold in the province. The new recruits included George Clarke, who proved to be a key instrument in bringing the gospel to the unreached minority groups of southwest China. Clarke's wife was the first foreign woman to live in Guizhou.

The first converts

As a trickle of Evangelical missionaries established themselves in Guizhou, it wasn't long before the first local believers emerged. In December 1881, two women based in Guiyang, Charlotte Kerr and Jane Kidd, reported that a growing number of women and children had started attending their meetings, and that "Three women appear thoroughly converted. Two of them are not yet baptized, but are longing to confess Christ in this way."[7]

A small school was set up in the mission home, and before long 13 children from extremely poor families were attending as boarders. The chief lesson taught each day was God's salvation, and the good news spread as students returned home and shared what they had learned with their families.

As the Holy Spirit moved, many students came under conviction for their sins. One day the oldest girl in the class refused to eat. When asked why, she replied that she was a terrible sinner and had lost her appetite.

The missionaries also established a clinic to help some of the many opium addicts in Guiyang. This work expanded quickly, and every man and woman who came for relief from the cursed

Jane Kidd, one of the first missionaries in Guizhou

drug was also presented with the gospel of salvation. In early 1882, Jane Kidd reported:

> One of our students' mothers spent several days here, and is cured of her opium smoking; she wishes to be baptized (as well as another woman), and I am sure she is sincere. The second woman, recently cured of opium smoking, comes very regularly for worship . . . In the case of our Miao woman . . . twice lately I have been filled with wonder at her. She is such a sweet Christian.
>
> If all at home who know about our working in this far-off province were to entreat God on behalf of the women of Guizhou, we should soon see a mighty gathering.[8]

Pressing into the kingdom

It appears Kidd's prayer request was acted upon, for within months the influence of the mission greatly increased in Guiyang. The deliverance of opium addicts was the talk of the town, for people believed it was impossible to be set free from the drug. As a result, dozens of inquirers came to hear about Jesus. One evening, Kidd was sharing the gospel at her home, when the number of inquirers grew so large that:

> About 100 women with children were inside, and more than that number were outside wishing to come in. As there were a number of men about, we dared not open our doors. They knocked very loudly and I feared they would break open the doors, but after asking help from God the men listened to persuasion and gradually went off. The women inside were prisoners for a time, and heard more of the glorious message than perhaps otherwise they would have done.[9]

Another strategy employed by the missionaries was to attend crowded markets and festivals, where they set up stalls and sold gospel literature at cost price to those who desired to know the truth. The message of Christ's salvation began to spread throughout the province as the missionaries and local believers visited new towns and counties. In one three-month period in 1882, evangelists "visited seven cities, and a large number of towns and villages . . . disposing of 1,940 gospels and portions of Scripture, 49 New Testaments, and about 1,000 Christian books and tracts."[10]

Chen Xiguang

The honor of being both the first Chinese Evangelical believer and the first Chinese pastor in Guizhou fell to a former Confucian scholar named Chen Xiguang, whose wife was a member of the Dong minority group. Chen first met missionaries Broumton and Landale in the spring of 1878, when the foreigners were seeking a language teacher. For a year they shared the gospel with Chen, but he showed no interest and refused to attend any of the Christian meetings.

Chen Xiguang—the first Evangelical Christian and pastor in Guizhou

The biggest stumbling block for Chen—and millions of Chinese inquirers in subsequent generations—was the fear of others and the powerful influence of ancestor worship. Chen was an only son and was thus responsible for upholding family traditions. He felt that if he became a Christian he would bring shame on his ancestors and family members.

In 1880, Chen was finally convicted of his sins and made a firm decision to follow Jesus Christ. He tore down the ancestral tablets and the tablet to Heaven and Earth from his wall, and began to attend the church services regularly. When members of Chen's family discovered that he had become a Christian they fiercely opposed him, but from the beginning Chen's walk with God was consistent, and he developed a great hunger to know and obey the Scriptures.

When Jane Kidd opened her school for girls in Guiyang, Chen was employed as the teacher. Each day after class was dismissed, he joined the missionaries in sharing the gospel with unbelievers, and he soon proved to be a bold and effective evangelist. For a time, Chen was the only native preacher in the entire province, and he was able to earn people's respect because of his standing as a Confucian scholar who was well versed in the Chinese classics. In 1896 it was said of Chen Xiguang:

> He is a little man, quiet and unassuming, and a splendid Chinese scholar. He is a true Christian and an earnest worker. He seems specially fitted for the work of an evangelist, his language in preaching being clear and simple. He can make himself understood by the most illiterate, and has a happy way of suiting himself and his subject to his hearers.[11]

Although Chen's wife resisted the gospel for years, she finally yielded to God and became the first Evangelical Christian among the Dong people. In time, the couple's children and relatives also came to Christ. While Chen's fellow believers loved and appreciated him deeply, he had one unusual flaw which caused concern. According to a report:

> His one failing is his drowsiness. Sometimes it seems impossible to keep him awake. He will fall asleep at morning meeting, at noon meeting, at afternoon meeting, at evening meeting, when teaching the foreigners, or when alone in the street chapel! He says this sleepiness is a disease, and truly it seems as if it is.
>
> We can overlook it, however. He has won his way to all our hearts and we love him as a brother. His untiring efforts to bring his fellow countrymen to Christ often stimulate us in our work, and we trust that he may be spared for many years to continue his labors of love in the church at Guiyang.[12]

Stalled progress

The tiny missionary force in Guizhou was deeply saddened when the highly effective Jane Kidd unexpectedly passed away in 1885, just four years after arriving in the province. Her absence was sorely felt, and the CIM work took a sudden turn to the worse, with just three baptisms recorded throughout the entire province in 1887, among a total number of only 25 church members.[13]

Although many people flocked to the chapels to hear the preaching of the gospel, few were willing to renounce their sins and dedicate their lives to Jesus Christ. Many of those who had taken the step of faith and been baptized had gradually fallen back into sin, and the Church was consequently struggling to make headway. One missionary lamented:

> Christian life has been at a very low ebb here the last two or three months. Some of the members have permitted the devil to get a hold of their hearts, and have apparently yielded to his temptations in many things, and there has been far from a spirit of brotherly love. Satan knows very well that a divided church is useless and a disgrace to God; it cannot work, and hinders many precious souls from entering the kingdom . . . Much prayer is needed that the light from the Church of God may be kept pure.[14]

In 1889, after 11 years of work in Guizhou, the CIM boasted just 37 believers in Guiyang and four in Anshun.[15] The remainder of the large province had failed to yield a single church member for the disillusioned missionaries.

By contrast, the Catholic work had experienced startling growth throughout Guizhou, with their membership leaping from 5,000 in 1886 to 16,900 believers in 73 churches in 1890.[16]

By the end of the 1880s the Evangelical enterprise in Guizhou had largely stalled, and both the missionaries and local believers wondered if there was any way forward. Few could have imagined that in the not-too-distant future, the living God would perform such an extraordinary work that thousands of people throughout the province would be forcing their way into the kingdom of God with joyful exuberance.

1890s

———•◦•———

Growth and persecution

The seed of the gospel had been slow to find fertile soil since the first Evangelical missionaries reached Guizhou in 1877, and by the early 1890s only a few individuals had come to the faith, and churches were few and far between. By 1893, the *China Mission Handbook* reported just 70 Evangelical Christians in the entire province, and a total of only 14 foreign missionaries, all of whom were serving with the China Inland Mission.[1]

Though small in number, most of the new believers encountered persecution from their families and communities, especially for their refusal to participate in ancestor worship rituals and their unwillingness to contribute money to the many idolatrous festivals held throughout the year.

As an example of the kind of persecution experienced by believers at the time, a man named Zhang was sharing the gospel with a group of youngsters as he walked home from a church service, when they turned on him and took his Bible and hymn book. Then suddenly:

> They pulled him down into the mud, and after kicking him about the head, departed. Zhang rose up and told the people that bad men had also ill-treated the Lord Jesus when He was on the earth ... The next day he met two of the men on the street, and asked if they had taken his Bible, or had only borrowed it. The men beat him again, and went on their way.[2]

Trouble at Panghai

In 1896 the CIM began to reach out to the many non-Chinese minority tribes in Guizhou. Fred and Ellen Webb were able to rent a house in the Hmu village of Panghai, near modern-day Kaili City. The Chinese were bemused as to why the foreigners would choose to live among the Hmu, as many Han at the time considered the tribespeople to be lower than dogs.

After gentle persuasion failed to make the missionaries leave the area, the leading Chinese official resorted to force, sending a mob of 150 men in an attempt to intimidate the Webbs. The experienced missionary Samuel Clarke was visiting Panghai at the time, and recalled the tense atmosphere:

> The Chinese headman of Panghai called upon us with the riff-raff of the village and the local robbers at their heels . . . They explained very elaborately that they personally had no objection to us, but the people were opposed to our remaining . . . Some of the rough fellows present, who had knives in their sleeves to emphasize what the headman had stated, said, "If you don't go away, we are going to beat you, pull down the house, and carry off your things."[3]

The missionaries refused to bow to the intimidation and remained where they were. The threats seemed to subside for a while until October 1898, when William Fleming of Scotland arrived to oversee the work at Panghai while the resident missionaries enjoyed a period of rest and recovery on the coast.

With a local Christian named Pan Xiushan acting as his interpreter, Fleming traveled widely among the Hmu for three weeks, preaching the gospel. While they were away from Panghai, the Hmu burned down 300 houses in the Chinese part of the village, in a protest over which day of the week the market should be held. Fleming decided to make his way to Guiyang and wait for the trouble to blow over, but he never made it.

William Fleming in Chinese clothes

On November 4, 1898, Fleming left for Guiyang accompanied by Pan Xiushan, an evangelist, and a man hired to carry their luggage. After traveling about 15 miles (24 km), they crossed a river on a hand-pulled raft, accompanied by three men, one of whom brandished a long sword. As they stepped onto the bank on the other side of the river:

> The people of the town streamed out along a road to see the devoted foreigner done to death . . . Just as they reached the bend where the road began to lead uphill, the man with the cavalry sword came behind the unsuspecting Pan Xiushan and struck him down, killing him almost instantly. He uttered a cry . . . Fleming struggled for some time with his assailants, but was finally done to death with many wounds.[4]

The murderers pursued the two other men before giving up the chase. Several days later the evangelist reached Guiyang and reported how Fleming and Pan had been murdered. Two

*William Fleming's grave, behind the old mission house at Panghai, is now
in a field overgrown with pumpkins and weeds*
Miao Messenger

missionaries, with an official escort, immediately left to recover
the bodies of the slain Christians. They found them unburied
on the side of the road.

It was later revealed that the murders of Fleming and Pan
occurred because of a false report that the missionaries had
been importing weapons and ammunition to help the Hmu
overthrow the Chinese, and the burning of homes by the Hmu
in Panghai had strengthened the rumors. After the two innocent Christians were killed, the locals immediately attempted
to find evidence to justify their claims, "but when they searched

Fleming's luggage, and ransacked his house, they found no arms, nothing but good books. He was certainly a good man and it was a mistake to kill him."[5]

William Fleming was the first ever martyr of the CIM. God had supernaturally protected its hundreds of workers during the 33 years since Hudson Taylor founded the mission.

The Hmu

Evangelical work among the multifaceted Miao people of Guizhou was slow to commence. The first missionaries settled in the province in 1877, and although they made immediate contact with the Miao, it wasn't until 20 years later in 1897 that a base was established in their midst. At the time, to reach Panghai from the provincial capital meant a perilous journey, passing through isolated areas inhabited by leopards and wolves.

Yong Gong, an 81-year-old Hmu man who was baptized at Panghai

The Hmu tribe is the largest of approximately 40 Miao ethnic groups in Guizhou. The people, in their own language, go by the name Hmu, but they were commonly labeled Hei Miao ("Black Miao") by the Chinese and missionaries because of the color of the women's dresses. The Hmu also speak their own language, distinct from other Miao varieties. After moving into the Hmu area in 1897, Ellen Webb joyfully wrote:

> We are now, by the grace of God, in the Hmu country, right among the people. The Lord Almighty opened a door, and enabled us to come in just at a time when clouds seemed to be gathering . . .
>
> The Hmu here are most friendly, and come around us freely, and we have every facility for learning the language . . . The people are anxious for me to wear their dress; as soon as the weather gets a little cooler I intend to put it on. The Hmu are not as inquisitive as the Chinese, and do not crowd around in the same way; they come and look and pass on. I like them very much; one feels more at ease with them than with the Chinese. Pray much for us, that we may remain here and, in God's time, that other workers may be sent, but, above all, that God will open the hearts of this people.[1]

Pan Xiushan—the first Hmu Christian and martyr

Pan Xiushan, a Hmu tribesman, was born and raised in Huangping, about 93 miles (150 km) east of Guiyang. His job as a mason frequently took him to the provincial capital, where Pan and his wife heard the gospel, believed and were baptized.

When Pan taught his Hmu language to a few of the missionaries, they were surprised to discover that the Miao languages in Guizhou differed markedly from each other. Little to nothing of the Hmu language could be understood by other Miao groups closer to Guiyang.[2]

Pan Xiushan, a Hmu martyr for Christ

Reports frequently mentioned the impact that Pan's preaching had on his fellow Hmu. A letter from Samuel Clarke in August 1899 noted:

> From early morning till 10:30 or 11:00 p.m. the chapel has been filled, and preaching has gone on all day. The evening service is a sight to behold; the place is packed inside, and as many people outside. Both Pan and the teacher [Henry Bolton] have preached splendidly, taking the meeting in turns. Every Sunday we have a room packed with men and children . . .[3]

The murders of William Fleming and Pan Xiushan sent shock-waves throughout the Hmu area. Pan was the first Hmu Christian; the people knew that he had died unjustly, and many pondered the message he had fearlessly preached. On May 12, 1899, little more than six months after the murders, a missionary wrote:

> There are quite a few persons in Panghai and Qingping who profess to be interested in the gospel and want their names put down as enquirers. Several parties have come to Guiyang to see us. One was deputed by 40 or 50 men and another by a whole village of 30 or 40 families. Already our brother's life and labors are bearing fruit.[4]

Over the next 18 months, a number of Hmu men and women professed faith in Jesus after understanding more of the gospel, and village leaders declared that large numbers of their people were ready to become Christians. Although many of the inquirers had no more than a basic grasp of Christian doctrine, great hopes were held that the Hmu were on the verge of a mass turning to Christ.

A turning point for evil

The work among the Hmu appeared to be on the cusp of a great breakthrough in 1900, when a fierce persecution broke out against the fledgling church which shook the confidence of the Hmu. The persecution was so destructive that its effects were long-lasting; it could be argued that Christianity has been resisted by the Hmu people as a harmful and dangerous influence to the present time.

The genesis of the persecution was born in the summer of 1900, when the Hmu grew tired of having their rice fields raided by Han settlers. The authorities did nothing to resolve the situation, so a mob of more than 200 Hmu bandits attacked the Chinese town of Kaili on the night of November 14, 1900. They set fire to more than a hundred houses, killed some military and government officials, and made off with the plunder.

At daybreak the bandits stopped at the village of Sanglang, near Panghai, where they ordered the people to feed them breakfast and threatened to shoot them if they refused. Sanglang at the time contained dozens of Hmu Christian families and inquirers.

After recovering from the surprise attack, the Chinese authorities plotted their revenge. They desired to spill much Hmu blood in order to "save face" from the humiliation. At the same time, some Hmu village headmen, sensing an opportunity to rid themselves of the hated Christians, falsely reported that the believers at Sanglang were behind the rebellion, and that the whole village had helped the bandits escape and had even provided breakfast for them on the morning after the raid.

The magistrate at Kaili hauled the Hmu family leaders of Sanglang—both Christians and non-Christians—off to court. When the judges appeared and interrogated the men:

> The officials were completely in the hands of the Hmu headmen, who acted as both accusers and interpreters. Not one in four of the accused could understand the magistrates, nor could the magistrates understand the accused . . . As a result, eight men from Sanglang, and 24 from other villages who had attended services at Panghai were put to death, some of them after they had been cruelly tortured for days in order that they might confess themselves to be rebel leaders.[5]

When news of the massacre reached the CIM headquarters, James Adam, a Scottish missionary, traveled from his base in Anshun to investigate the case. He reported:

> These poor persecuted ones meekly marched off into the town. Days before this they had their homes looted of everything—grain, farming implements, and household utensils . . . As soon as they reached the Intendant's presence, eight of their number were set apart and seven of them beheaded right away; no trial or any inquiry![6]

Most of the slain men were elderly village leaders who were numbered among the first Hmu Christians. A few years earlier, some of them had dug the graves to lay the bodies of the martyred Pan Xiushan and William Fleming, and now others came to dig their graves.

Still not placated, the authorities sent soldiers to 20 different villages, determined to root out all Christian influence and to leave the believers destitute by plundering their possessions. Family heads were ordered to sign a form denouncing Christianity, and were forced to pay a fine. Thirty-six families signed the forms, although they later told Adam, "They said that we recanted, but in our hearts we did no such thing. It was only the money they wanted."[7]

Afterwards, an investigation was conducted; it concluded that not a single Christian had been involved in the looting of Kaili, but it was too late for the 34 men who had been slain for crimes they didn't commit.[8] One of the martyrs, an elderly man named Wang Jinting, was falsely accused of being a bandit. He was held for five days without food and tortured mercilessly in order to extract a confession. When he was ordered to kneel before the magistrate:

> He exhorted his son with many good words to serve God and to do his duty, and he spoke of his trust in the Lord Jesus . . . His son, when at the market in Kaili, heard that some Christians were being taken out for beheading. He ran and was in time to see his dear old father led out. He could not get near to speak to him and was much afraid lest they should recognize him and kill him too. Poor lad, he wept as he related his father's sufferings.[9]

The hardening of the Hmu

For a time the missionaries were encouraged that the remaining Hmu believers appeared to be steadfast, but the cruel martyrdoms and persecution, instead of causing the churches to flourish and grow, put fear into the hearts of most Hmu and created resistance toward Christianity. Many people were unable to reconcile the fact that God had not rescued his followers in their time of distress, and subsequent generations of Hmu have generally turned their backs on the gospel.

Fallout from the massacre continued to reverberate with negative effects among the Hmu population for decades. The long-serving Australian missionaries Maurice and Stella Hutton, who led the CIM work among the Hmu for decades, described the cool reception they received at a village 14 years later:

> Some of the men began to curse my men for leading us to their village. They did not want the foreigner nor his gospel, for some years earlier, they said, all those who had anything to do with the Gospel Hall were killed.[10]

Even in 1937, nearly four decades after the massacre, the Huttons reported, "To this day many are afraid to have anything to do with the gospel for fear of the threats which officials still make of repeating this same treatment of Christians."[11]

A faithful remnant

One reason the work among the Hmu never prospered appears to be because efforts to reach them were too thinly spread, with the handful of missionaries in eastern Guizhou scattering the seed of the gospel not only among the Hmu but also among the Dong, Ge, Shui, Gelao, Mulao Jia and other tribes in the region. Because of this diluted strategy, the gospel failed to find fertile soil. Few Hmu really understood the Christian message, and in most years only a few Hmu people were baptized.

Life became extremely difficult in the Hmu areas during the 1920s and 1930s, with bandits causing anarchy and much loss of life. To make matters worse, a typhoid epidemic struck in 1927, killing many people. Because of the large number of decomposing corpses in the towns, packs of hungry wolves came out of the mountains. Maurice Hutton noted the grim situation facing the Hmu Christians at the time:

Our night meetings are very poorly attended . . . Many members are sick, and others have to wait upon the sick so they cannot come. Moreover, the scare nowadays of wolves rushing down the hills into the city street and carrying off children, goats, live persons and dead bodies, keeps many people at home, for needless to say, unless people can go in companies at night they are too fearful to venture out to attend meetings.[12]

Despite the many challenges, God preserved a small remnant of faithful Hmu disciples, and in 1927 Hutton noted, "The work is decidedly growing in the Hmu district. There is one Christian village, and if only the foreign missionaries could be permanently settled among this people I believe the work would show signs of rapid growth."[13] The following year Hutton was encouraged by developments:

Truly it is remarkable to see how firmly these tribal people stand, though left alone without a resident missionary for so long . . . Each company of believers is carrying on their Lord's Day and weekday services. A very good feature of the work among these Hmu is that they are marrying and intermarrying between villages where gospel services are held, and so this more intimate family relationship springing up between them is resulting in constant visits being paid, and so encouraging themselves the more in their most holy faith.[14]

One of the key figures in the Hmu Church for many years was a man named Ah So (whose Chinese name was Pan Desheng). He had been born the third son of a spirit-priest, and Hmu tradition demanded that he be sacrificed as an infant to appease the demons. At the sacrifice, however, a pig's body was substituted for his own, and his life was spared.

After becoming a Christian, Ah So traveled extensively throughout the area, visiting hundreds of villages and distributing thousands of gospel tracts and books to interested people. Hutton described Ah So as his "right-hand man" during 18 years of ministry among the Hmu.

Further progress occurred in 1930, after Maurice and Stella Hutton were finally permitted to reside again in the Hmu region after an absence of nine years. They joyfully reported:

> At first we had not a soul attending the meetings from the villages around. Prayer prevailed and now we have quite a goodly number at each Lord's Day service. At the many out-stations, the Christians carried on during the nine years without a missionary, and gradually they added to their numbers those who were saved. Before we had been back living among them for a year, the Lord gave us the joy of seeing 15 people baptized . . . This, our second year back among them, the Lord has done even greater things, for already 25 men and women have been baptized, and we hope there will be a few more before this year closes . . . It is the Lord's doing and we rejoice in Him and take courage for the future.[15]

Like a seed slowly sprouting into life, a strong body of believers appeared to be emerging among the Hmu. By 1937 Hutton summarized the influence of the mission with these words:

> Although it is a work wherein souls are saved in the ones and twos, we have three organized churches, 13 out-stations, with schools, medical dispensary, colporteurs and voluntary preaching bands of men and women . . . We have even seen the devil-worshipping priests turn from devils to serve the Living God, tearing down every trace of devil worship from home and heart . . . Today we have Christians of the third and fourth generation of those men who, rather than give up their faith in Jesus, quietly knelt down and had their heads severed.[16]

Scriptures for the Hmu

Hutton also spearheaded efforts to translate the Bible into the Hmu language. There was no Hmu script, however, so the task was a complicated one. First, an orthography had to be created, and the people taught how to read it, before competent believers were chosen for the crucial translation process. Because the number of Hmu Christians was minuscule compared to the population, the challenge of finding enough people interested in reading the finished product created an added pressure.

Hutton threw himself into the translation, believing it would result in many thousands of Hmu accepting the gospel. In 1928, the first Hmu Scripture portions and a hymnal were printed, and the indefatigable Australian missionary continued to translate the New Testament one book at a time. Four years later he wrote:

> The Hmu New Testament translation has claimed the greater part of my time. Though this work has proved to be most exacting, yet to see one after the other of the books of the New Testament translated into the language of the Hmu . . . is a joy abundant which amply repays the labor put forth . . . For years it was useless almost to read from the Chinese New Testament in the services among the Hmu, for scarcely a soul understood what was being read . . . Now the people in the audience repeat the message from God's Word in their very own language.[17]

A sample of the phonetic script used for the Hmu New Testament

The Huttons relocated to Shandong Province to finish the translation work and to oversee the printing, but while there, they heard that many of the Hmu Christians had fallen away from the faith.

They were deeply discouraged to discover that even Ah So, their faithful co-worker of 18 years, had "married a heathen wife and had gone back in his zeal. He had even given up reading God's Word and prayer, and decided to leave us and the Lord's work."[18]

The entire Hmu New Testament was finally completed in 1934, and the first books rolled off the press the following year. Unfortunately, the desire to read God's Word never gripped most Hmu people, and they continued to view Christianity as a dangerous foreign religion. Over time Hutton's translation largely fell into disuse, although in 1990 one researcher found it was still being used by a group of about 50 Hmu believers near Kaili.[19]

The dark decades

After the end of the Second World War, the Huttons wanted to move back to the Hmu region and rejoin the battle, but the CIM were not in agreement and considered the Huttons too old for the task (Maurice was in his late fifties at the time). In 1950 they were replaced by two American couples—Ivan and Mary Allbutt, and Ernie and Mertie Heimbach. With the Communists now in full control of the country, their missionary careers were short-lived. One of the final reports from the region, sent by a CIM worker, painted a grim assessment of the state of Hmu Christianity in Panghai:

> The spiritual side of the picture is dark indeed . . . Outwardly the people are friendly and seem genuinely happy to have us here. Nevertheless, in spiritual matters there is a strange aloofness. There is little real interest in the message we have come to bring, and they seem to find it a tremendous task to understand the barest essentials of the gospel . . .
>
> Of the Christians who at one time were attached to the church there only remains three or four who in any outward

way confess His Name. Even they are miserably weak and stand in need of reviving grace. A few others are back in the thralls of demonology and sin. They give no evidence of ever having had life, although they used to attend when former missionaries were here. There is no Christian here to whom we can look for companionship and help in the work . . .

Praise God, some of the Hmu church leaders from other centers have been to visit us recently and they are a tremendous encouragement. We had blessed prayer fellowship with them and it was with rejoicing that we saw them standing firm on the Rock with faith and courage. I pray the Lord might raise up men of their calibre here in Panghai itself.[20]

The Heimbachs were expelled from Panghai in February 1951, just three months after commencing their missionary calling. The Allbutts were also arrested and removed from China by the Communist regime, and a dark curtain was drawn on the long, yet largely fruitless, work among the Hmu.

Tellingly, in his final communication before being expelled, Ivan Allbutt wrote a summary of the more than 50 years of efforts to penetrate the Hmu with the gospel. He referenced the massacres of Hmu Christians in 1900, and how "three generations later, it is still a hindrance to the preaching of the gospel among this tribe." He sadly concluded:

In a tribe conservatively estimated to include 500,000 people, there are about 100 who have confessed the Lord in baptism, with perhaps that many more who have made some sign of interest in Christian things. One hundred among half a million.

There has been no resident missionary among this tribe at all, for any length of time, since 1934. They have the New Testament in their language, but are still waiting for some missionaries to teach them how to use it.[21]

The Hmu today

Today, more than a century has passed since the massacre of Hmu Christians, but the people have never been fully able to shrug off those wicked events, and the Hmu remain one of the largest unreached people groups in China. One contemporary source estimates that only about 7,000 (or less than 0.5 percent) of the three million Hmu people are Christians today.[22]

Though the Hmu Christians are not large in number, they have continued to hold onto their faith in Jesus, even as the flame has flickered very dimly at times.

The last few decades have witnessed a dramatic shift in the demographics of the Hmu. Hundreds of villages in eastern Guizhou have been depopulated, some almost completely, as people of working age flee the poverty and lack of opportunities

A Hmu church near Kaili. A handful of elderly believers in this congregation still read the Scriptures translated by Maurice Hutton in 1934
Miao Messenger

and migrate to the large cities in search of work. Many do not return except on special occasions like the Chinese New Year. Consequently, many Hmu villages today consist of elderly people taking care of their grandchildren, while all the men and women of working age are absent.

May God's people everywhere cry out in fervent prayer for the salvation of the gentle yet traumatized Hmu people of Guizhou. May the living God have mercy on them, and complete the wonderful plan He had begun to implement before Satan and wicked men intervened to shut the hearts of generations of Hmu to the claims of the gospel.

1900s

Decay in Guiyang

At the start of the twentieth century, the gospel was being proclaimed to the Han Chinese living in the main cities of Guizhou,
but very few had responded to the message. Surprisingly, the
China Inland Mission continued to be the only Evangelical
group working in the province. Whereas denominations like
the Presbyterians, Methodists, Anglicans, Baptists and others
had thriving work in other parts of China, they chose to avoid
Guizhou, leaving the entire province in the hands of the small
and understaffed CIM. In 1902 one missionary wrote from
Guiyang:

> We are encouraged that interest in the meetings on the part
> of both men and women shows no sign yet of declining. The
> numbers who attend the meetings seem to be on the increase.
> On the evenings of Tuesday and Friday the number of men who
> come ranges from 40 to 60 . . . Some have put away their idols,
> to whose removal they were at the time very much opposed.[1]

Just a year later, however, the work in Guiyang reached a low
ebb, with the CIM lamenting, "There have been no baptisms
during the year, but, on the contrary, four members have had to
be excluded from fellowship, one has died, and two have been
transferred to other stations."[2]

Two thousand families deferred in Dushan

In the south Guizhou county of Dushan—at the time a six-day
journey from the provincial capital—a delegation of ten village

61

Thomas Windsor

leaders approached missionary Thomas Windsor in 1902, claiming they each had between 50 and 500 families under their charge who were ready to be baptized and admitted into the Church.

The missionary wisely exercised caution, however, and he soon discovered that most of the "believers" had no understanding of the gospel at all. Their motives for wanting to become Christians were mixed, but chief among them was a hope that being connected to foreigners would earn them protection from their Chinese oppressors. This idea stemmed from observing Catholic churches in the province, which vigorously supported their members in lawsuits, and occasionally even threatened the use of foreign force during major disputes. Windsor reported:

> I think they were disappointed that I did not jump at the chance offered . . . Being disappointed in these expectations, one or two showed me a cool front. That, however, is a small matter so long as their minds are disabused of such dangerous and erroneous notions . . . While being polite and friendly, I nevertheless did

my best to be perfectly straightforward with them, so as to obviate trouble in the future. Altogether there were more than 2,000 families who were willing to join us.[3]

Although the Dushan village leaders returned home disappointed, the missionaries realized that if the people were able to gain a true understanding of the gospel, including the requirements of repentance and the need to forsake idolatry, a major movement to Jesus Christ might follow. They saw the incident at Dushan not as a rebuttal of hungry inquirers, but rather as a necessary delay to allow people's understanding of the faith to catch up with their zeal for change.

By 1905, however, no mass movement to Christ had occurred in Dushan. It appears the village leaders were put off by the offense of the cross, and they never again offered their people to become Christians. Notwithstanding, some individuals at Dushan did respond to the good news, among them an elderly woman who received the Lord with great joy.

James Adam and the Anshun mission

James Adam—the Scottish missionary who led the CIM station at Anshun—had arrived in China in 1887, at the age of 23. He felt deeply discouraged by his initial years trying to reach Han people in Guizhou, and he struggled to see any way forward in the work. Then, in August 1894, he was devastated by the sudden death of his Canadian wife, who perished from fever just two days after giving birth to a baby girl. Adam rushed home to find his beloved wife already lying in a coffin. His little daughter also died soon after.

Adam was struck to the core, and told the local believers:

When my wife was in Guiyang she was told that it would be dangerous for her to live in Anshun because of the malaria; yet she was willing to go, hoping to help you women trust in Jesus.

James Adam

God asks my all, my wife, my babe; He gave them to me; I willingly let Him take them back.[4]

Adam was able to muster the courage to write a letter on the day after the funeral:

I laid my darling wife and precious wee babe in the grave yesterday morning. This is such a sudden plunge into deepest affliction, that at first I felt crushed, but now, I can truly say with my glorified wife: "I am pleased with God's will." This was one of the precious things she said before she fell asleep in Jesus . . .

The Christians have all shown great sympathy . . . but the greatest comfort to me was that wee Mary was a living babe. But alas the Lord saw fit to take her from me too, so that He has taken all . . . This is indeed a sore trial, but the Lord is having mercy upon me, and I can say, "Though he slays me yet will I trust in Him!"

As I told the crowd yesterday at the grave, Jesus can heal broken hearts, and He would heal mine. Pray for me and for our relations that God may bind up our grief and that I may truly profit by this greatest of trials.[5]

After a period of grieving, Adam visited Britain in 1896, where he met with the great mission leader Hudson Taylor. When Adam asked how he could possibly share the gospel with both the Chinese and the Miao, Taylor responded, "Go on, dear brother, and do the best you can for both."

Upon returning to China, Adam expanded his work, visiting every Miao village in a 15 mile (25 km) radius from Anshun. Over time, he visited 250 different Miao villages and built relationships with many community leaders.

James Adam, who remarried in 1897,[6] discovered that in addition to having suffered centuries of abuse at the hands of the Chinese, the Miao were plagued by malaria, resulting in the deaths of thousands of people each year. Moreover, the hot summer months brought infectious skin diseases, which cast many onto a bed of suffering. All of these factors combined to humble the Miao of Anshun, leaving them with little pretension or self-righteousness.

The mission obtained a supply of medicine and ointment to treat malaria and skin diseases, and a steady flow of thankful people developed a deep respect for the servants of the gospel. The first believers in Anshun were baptized in 1898, and the following year a chapel and a Christian school for boys were opened. The school turned out to be a key to advancing the gospel. One source noted that "Adam successively took in a group of poor Miao children and orphans for studies . . . Within less than a year he could speak the Miao language of several dialect areas."[7]

Anshun proved to be a strategic center for the Miao work, with members of many different tribes passing through the area, both for commerce and during migrations to other areas.

As a result, many Miao tribes had settled in the districts surrounding the city. All the groups shared a common historic kinship, but had evolved over many centuries to possess their own languages, dress and customs. The tribes considered themselves distinct from one another, and youngsters were often forbidden from intermarrying with other Miao.

Adam's writings referred to various tribal names, but it appears the two largest Miao groups he encountered in the early years of his ministry were the Hua Miao and the Hmong Shua. Other tribes inhabiting the districts around Anshun included the A-Hmao, Hmong Daw, Hmong Leng, Hmong Njua, and a small number of Hmu people who had migrated into the area from further east.

The Chinese labeled these groups by names that described the women's clothing. For example, the A-Hmao were known as the Da Hua ("Big Flowery") Miao, the Hmong Daw as Bai ("White") Miao, the Hmu as Hei ("Black") Miao, and the Hmong Leng as Hongtou ("Red Hat" or "Red-Headed") Miao.

Three more tribes mentioned by Adam within reach of Anshun included the "Wooden Comb" Miao, the Shuixi ("West of the River") Miao, and the Shui ("Water") Miao. These three tribes are all considered part of the Hmong Shua language group today.

The CIM workers were thrilled whenever they came across a new tribe. They appreciated each group's unique characteristics and realized they were created by God and precious in his sight.

The King of the Miao

Many of the Miao tribes shared a common belief that they had once possessed a written language, but when the Chinese drove them from the fertile plains into the barren mountains of south China they had tried to cross a deep river, and sadly the strong current swept many people away and their sacred books were destroyed. A pastor, Wang Mingji, expressed how the Miao people felt about having no written language:

> For thousands of years we have been like the blind. It has been very bitter. Everybody knows that there is nothing worse in the world than to be blind. However shimmering is the sun in the sky, however shimmering is the moon, however clear are the rivers and the mountains on the earth, however beautiful are the flowers in the wilderness, the blind cannot see them.[8]

A widespread legend persisted that one day a "King of the Miao" would come and return their written language to them. Many were astonished to discover that a white man was able to speak several Miao languages. When James Adam began translating the Bible and teaching them how to read, many people were convinced that he was the long-awaited Miao king.

In 1903, a prominent Miao leader named Li Matai even summoned the people of his village and sacrificed an ox. At the ceremony, he proclaimed, "There has appeared a Miao king in Anshun. He is very affectionate and kind-hearted to the Miao. He calls us his brothers, and he helps ordinary hard-working Miao as much as possible."[9]

Veteran missionary William Hudspeth described the impact made by the arrival of the first Miao Scriptures:

> When the British and Foreign Bible Society sent the first Gospels and these were distributed the legend grew—the once-upon-a-time lost books had been found in the white man's country, and they told the incomparable story that Jesus loved the Miao. Only the imagination can conceive what this meant to those hillsmen, some of whom travelled for days to view the books.[10]

Mission work in Guizhou was put on hold in 1900 when the Boxer Rebellion broke out throughout China. Adam was ordered to evacuate to the coast until the uprising subsided. When he returned to Anshun in 1901, Adam found that only a few dozen Miao believers were still faithfully following God, but a year later he had the joy of baptizing more than 20 new Hua Miao converts, some of whom became his eager assistants, tirelessly spreading the gospel to as many villages as possible. The magazine *China's Millions* broke the wonderful news that at Anshun, "Sixty-one Miao were baptized in the presence of between 1,000 and 2,000 of their fellow tribesmen . . . many of whom have been coming to the services at Anshun once a month for more than two years."[11]

Revival breaks out

The awakening among the Hua Miao near Anshun soon spread to other tribes in the region. The first to benefit was a group

Four Hmong Shua Christian women at Anshun

known in Chinese as the Shui ("Water") Miao, who called themselves Hmong Shua in their own language. Adam wrote of his first contact with this group:

> To reach their district a river has to be crossed. For a long time no Miao would take me over that river, as they said the Chinese would kill them if they did so. At last, however, I found that a Miao evangelist had a relative who had married into the Hmong Shua tribe. Through this man and his wife I secured an introduction to the tribe over the river.[12]

On the second day of Adam's visit with the Hmong Shua, a man suddenly died while working in his field. Adam immediately went and shared the gospel with the villagers, and the Lord granted him favor. At the start of 1907, Adam announced:

> The work quickly spread from village to village, and before long we had people from scores of villages attending the services at Anshun. Later we built a chapel and opened an out-station at Dengdeng. The Miao gave the site—trees for pillars, and stone for building, also money and free labor. Now there are at Dengdeng about 64 church members, and 200 to 300 people attending the services on Sundays.[13]

A Hmong Shua schoolteacher was given a Chinese copy of the Gospel of Luke and a hymn book. After returning home, he familiarized himself with the contents of the books and began teaching them to his students. He then gathered the entire village together and taught them the gospel. As a result, one day Adam returned home from a long journey to find a group of men waiting for him. They demanded the missionary come to their village immediately. That night as Adam prepared to sleep, he was told a bonfire would be lit in the morning. After sunrise, everyone gathered in the center of the village. Adam later described what happened:

The drums used in sacrifice and sorcerer's wands and other instruments and charms were thrown into the fire. One woman said, "Why should I wear this lucky charm? I now trust in the Living God. The sorcerer told me to wear this. I shall trust his lies no longer," and she threw it into the fire. All the other women followed her example. They ran to their houses and brought out all the "soul-packets" they had [charms to ward off evil spirits]. These we also threw into the fire.[14]

At the first baptismal service, nine Hmong Shua converts passed from death to life and became the first ever believers among their group. The following spring 20 more men and women were baptized in that village.

The blessing spreads to the A-Hmao

One day while he was staying at Dengdeng village, Adam was surprised to see a group of Miao men returning from a boar hunt. They were covered in dirt and had their hair twisted around their heads in the shape of a horn. In all his travels Adam had never encountered this group before, and he was excited to discover the men were from the A-Hmao tribe.

Most of the A-Hmao people lived nine days' walk from Anshun, across numerous mountains and deep valleys. The people had so greatly multiplied in their home territory that the land could no longer support their numbers, so several hundred families had migrated south.

The A-Hmao had been oppressed for countless generations and they had little dignity left. They were considered the lowest rung on the social ladder, and a landlord "would mount his horse by stepping on the back of a stooping A-Hmao . . . The landlords would sell A-Hmao women as slaves or wives and frequently tortured the men."[15]

A group of A-Hmao Christian women at Anshun in 1906

Although James Adam didn't know it at the time, his chance encounter with the hunters was the start of the largest and most powerful people movement to Christ among all the tribes of Guizhou. The missionaries at Anshun suddenly found themselves in the midst of a full-blown revival, and each day was filled with extraordinary experiences of the glory of God. Adam recalled that when an old man first understood the gospel, he proclaimed:

> "It is not good for us to keep such good news to ourselves. Let us go and tell our kinsmen!" . . . The old man at once went and told the people about the Lord Jesus Christ . . . The people from that village came down in great numbers to Anshun to see us, at first several times a month and later regularly once a month.[16]

The A-Hmao were hungry to learn more about the living God, so they dispatched delegations to Anshun to soak in all they could about the new faith. Such was their intense desire for the gospel that many made the long journey of nine or ten days each way over steep mountains and through deep rivers.

Because the Chinese despised the A-Hmao and refused to let them stay at their inns or eat in their restaurants, the pilgrims were forced to carry all their food in goatskin bags during their arduous journeys. They slept under the stars at night, braving the conditions because the kingdom of God had become a pearl of great price to them, and no sacrifice was too great to make.

Adam and his wife felt overwhelmed by the steady stream of people who came to visit. They wrote: "Our house was just crowded out with them. One night I went round and counted my guests. We had over 300 sleeping in the house. Still they came from more and more distant places. This continued for months."[17]

Stone Gateway

As the revival continued to spread, Adam and his Miao co-workers asked a group of A-Hmao visitors from a distant place if they were familiar with the town of Zhaotong in neighboring Yunnan Province, where another missionary from Scotland, the Methodist Samuel Pollard, had established an effective work. Adam was surprised when they answered that Zhaotong was only two or three days' walk from their home village, compared to the nine days it had taken them to reach Anshun. Adam encouraged the shy tribesmen to visit Pollard. They were hesitant at first, but finally agreed to go, and were warmly received.

The connection with Zhaotong proved to be a great boost for the advancement of the gospel among the A-Hmao. Pollard was soon overwhelmed with hundreds of inquirers just as Adam had been, and within a short time more than a thousand

A-Hmao converts were baptized. Pollard later described this stunning development:

> If anyone had to choose a people to teach and train, surely he would pass by these A-Hmao, and select a people whose outlook seemed more promising. So we think. So does not God think. He often does a startling thing, a new thing. The serfs in the dirty villages, the poor in the homes of poverty, the ignorant in the grip of the wicked medicine men—these appealed to the love and sympathy and chivalry of the Great God . . . The people knew nothing of God and never cried to Him. But God knew them, and the time for His working came.[18]

An A-Hmao chief donated a piece of land at Shimenkan (meaning "Stone Gateway"), 23 miles (37 km) from Zhaotong. A large church building and school were constructed, which served as the center of both A-Hmao and Nosu Christianity for many years. All the money, material and labor for the buildings was provided by the local believers.

The work among the A-Hmao grew spectacularly, with thousands of people regularly attending church services. It was reported:

> Deep interest is manifested in the gospel, with the audiences on three successive Sundays being about 900, 1,000, and 1,300 respectively. An early morning prayer meeting was held at which nearly 500 women were present, a number of whom lifted up their voices in public prayer to God.[19]

Persecution fails to stop the advance

As with all genuine moves of God throughout history, Satan soon tried to hinder the A-Hmao revival. Wicked people rose up against the new faith, attacking and robbing believers as they traveled, and the Chinese falsely accused them of poisoning wells that they passed during their long treks to and from Anshun. The greatest opposition, however, arose from within the A-Hmao communities. As Adam reported, their own tribal chiefs and spirit-priests, fearing a loss of influence as people abandoned their former ways and embraced new life in Christ, "had many of the Christians cast into prison, beaten, and fined. They also threatened to deprive of their land all who continued to read our books, or joined themselves to us."[20]

The persecution was most severe in western Guizhou, but it soon petered out as the sheer weight of numbers of A-Hmao people coming to the Lord overwhelmed and blunted the opposition. Many meetings at Kopu were attended by between two and three thousand eager tribespeople, and baptisms of hundreds of new converts were regularly conducted. James Adam described the A-Hmao believers' unquenchable zeal for God:

> They go out two by two visiting the villages far and near, preaching, singing and praying. Often when visiting these villages my heart has been delighted at the eager way in which the people seek to learn and gain the most benefit from the visit, even if it is only for one night. They will sit up listening till one or two o'clock in the morning. Frequently I have retired at that hour and at daylight have awakened to find them still learning to read texts of Scripture or some hymn of praise, or perhaps giving earnest heed to one of the Christians.[21]

As they traveled around the A-Hmao villages, Adam and his co-workers customarily used a kerosene lantern to project images of Bible stories onto the wall of any suitable building. The tribespeople often watched transfixed as the life, death and resurrection of Christ was presented and explained to them. At one village, when they came to the betrayal and crucifixion, Adam recalled:

> A great hush and silence fell upon the crowd . . . Many in the great congregation were weeping, and I myself could not keep

back the tears . . . Next day 240 communicants sat round the Lord's table breaking bread and drinking the cup, thus showing the Lord's death till He comes. It was a glorious scene and my heart overflowed with praise to God at the sight of so many who recently were devil worshippers and sunken in immorality and sin, but who are now among His blood-washed ones.[22]

The revival among the A-Hmao had appeared suddenly, and it burned with such intensity that the missionaries and their helpers had no way of keeping up with the progress. Throughout the hills of Guizhou, thousands of men and women who had been crushed and despised for countless generations now found their worth in their Creator, Jesus Christ.

Baptisms from morning till night

When news of the A-Hmao revival reached Britain and America, some Christians there were skeptical, and they wondered if the reports were exaggerated. The missionaries were instructed to ensure that all candidates for baptism thoroughly understood and believed the truths of the Gospels before being accepted into the Church. Mission boards even dispatched workers from other parts of China to verify the reports of the revival in Guizhou.

One missionary, Curtis Waters, was given the task of interviewing a large group of A-Hmao men and women who had applied to be baptized. Working each day from morning until late at night, Waters asked the candidates searching questions to ensure they were true believers. At first, many of the men and women were terrified by the examination of their doctrine and lives, as most had never spoken with a foreigner before. Waters filed this report:

A man came and sat on a stool before us with 20 or 30 members sitting behind him, and was asked a series of questions which embraced all the principal articles of doctrine—the person of God, the trinity, the incarnation, redemption, intercession, coming of Christ, together with matters relating to life and practice . . .

I went out into the chapel for something, and, coming back, I found a man waiting at the door with his face in his hands, praying. Afterwards I got to know that he had been waiting two or three days, and was afraid his village was not going to be called up . . .

Laughter and tears were very near each other as we listened to some of their replies and recognized the grace and power of God manifested in these people . . . Many came in and sat down trembling all over, wondering what questions they would be asked and whether they would be able to answer . . . There were many old men and women, 60, 70, and over, and it was a rare thing that any of them had to be deferred for not being clear on the doctrine. It was marvelous, and I noted many times how clear and decisive they were . . .

For eight days this continued to be our daily program: From nine till two I examined candidates for baptism, then baptismal service, evening meal, and, after meeting again, examining till midnight or one o'clock. We had eight days' baptisms as follows: 201, 131, 152, 95, 108, 142, 128 and 12; a total of 969 in all . . .

The work is unquestionably of the Holy Spirit. The utter impossibility of any man thus teaching all these people attests to it . . . These people, with an unquestioning faith simply accept the gospel teaching, and it is real to them. So, as ever, things hidden from the wise and learned He has revealed to babes. God has called them and revealed His Son in them, and to Him and the Word of His grace we commend them. He is able to keep them, and to make them the first-fruits of a multitude who shall yet be gathered out from this people to the praise and glory of His Name.[23]

An extraordinary decade

As the first decade of the twentieth century drew to a close, the body of Christ in Guizhou looked back in awe and marveled at what the almighty God had accomplished.

The decade, which started terribly with the slaughter of 34 Hmu Christians, had concluded with full-blown revival among several Miao tribes in the province. By contrast, the work among the Han Chinese in the urban centers had struggled to progress, despite the faithful efforts of many missionaries. In Guiyang, the Evangelical church had reached such a low ebb in 1905 that it was decided to disband the congregation and reorganize with a smaller membership.[24]

At the start of the decade there had been only 70 Evangelical believers in the entire province,[25] and by 1904 the number had grown to just 123.[26]

When James Adam returned from a furlough in 1909, however, he wrote from the village of Kopu: "On the Lord's Day several thousand A-Hmao attended the services, and about 900 sat around the table of the Lord . . . Connected with Kopu are 217 villages and hamlets; a Christian population of 7,000; and 2,000 communicants."[27]

The work continued to expand under the blessing of God, and Christian meetings were soon being held every night in hundreds of villages. By 1911, the influence of the Anshun mission had expanded so rapidly that they now served a total of 3,504 church members, 19 evangelists, 192 local leaders, 3 Biblewomen, and 13 schools.[28] Just a few years earlier, few people in Anshun had shown any interest in the gospel.

When the missionaries looked back several years after the revival began, they found that the Spirit of God had done a deep and lasting work. It was reported, "Of the 1,200 candidates baptized in 1906, we only know of three who have failed in trusting God."[29]

1910s

―――・●・――

A province divided

The new decade of the 1910s got underway with a promise of great things for the Church in Guizhou, although several barriers needed to be overcome for the gospel to gain widespread acceptance. A division existed between people living in the cities, where missionary progress had been excruciatingly slow, and those living in rural villages who were generally much more receptive to the claims of Christ.

A further division existed between western areas of Guizhou, where promising breakthroughs had occurred, and the eastern half of the province which remained spiritually barren with very few Christians and little gospel witness.

The most prominent division in Guizhou, however, occurred along ethnic lines. Some groups, including the Han Chinese, were adherents of organized religions such as Buddhism and Daoism, causing them to be more resistant to Christianity. On the other hand, the spirit- and nature-worshipping tribal animists appeared to have few hindrances to embracing Jesus Christ wholeheartedly once they heard the message in a clear manner.

In the 1910s, Guizhou was an anomaly among the provinces of China in that just one missionary organization, the CIM, almost exclusively worked in the province, although in the previous decade the Methodists had also established a base in northwest Guizhou. Other mission groups would soon arrive, giving an overall boost and helping spread the gospel to more people.

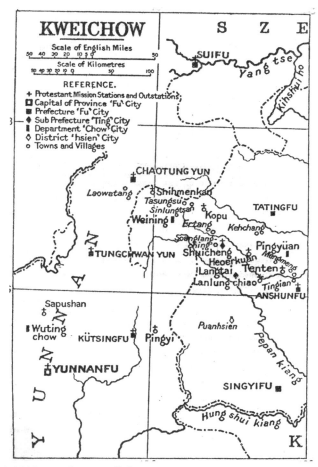

A 1910 map showing all the mission stations in western Guizhou

Dangers, toils and snares

The Qing Dynasty unraveled in 1911, and China was thrown into social disorder and lawlessness, with remote Guizhou not

Mrs. E. Adam (James's third wife) with a group of A-Hmao believers at Anshun in 1912

spared from the chaos. The missionaries and their converts began to encounter severe danger.

In 1911, five cities in Zunyi Prefecture staged an open rebellion against Chinese rule, with the people massacring a general and 200 of his troops. With the economy in complete disarray, thousands of men in Guizhou turned to banditry, robbing and murdering innocent victims. The lawlessness continued for many years before the authorities were finally able to get it under control.

Government leaders in Anshun were concerned for James Adams' safety, and they insisted that armed soldiers be sent to protect him on his travels. At first Adam resisted the idea, but he relented when the violence worsened. On the first few journeys, however, Adam discovered that the soldiers sent to accompany him were not used to trekking for days over high mountains, and they often lagged many miles behind. The missionary pressed on, only reconnecting with his "protectors" days later at prearranged stops along the way.

During one grueling six-week journey, Adam and his colleagues were tipped off that a massive group of five hundred bandits was hiding in a large cave near the road they intended to travel down the next day. They would have walked right into the ambush but for the help of local Christians, who led the missionaries on a long detour through another district to avoid the murderers.

All through that time of social chaos and turmoil, Adam's greatest concern was for the Miao churches. In 1912 he wrote:

> If the newly-interested Miao enquirers were only grounded in the Truth, persecution would, no doubt, help them, but they are for the most part only beginners, and one fears lest they should not stand firm in the face of such fierce opposition as they are called to endure. Over 1,000 families have been enrolled as enquirers. Please pray much for these dear, persecuted Miao enquirers.[1]

The Pollard script

As the gospel continued to flourish among the A-Hmao, it became apparent that the believers needed God's Word in their heart language if Christianity was ever going to make a lasting impact. Previously the A-Hmao believers had tried to read the Chinese Bible, but it was completely foreign to most of them, and it consequently failed to impact their hearts or change their lives.

The gifted James Adam found himself at the forefront of a new initiative to translate God's Word into A-Hmao. He began

Samuel Clarke in 1916

work in 1908, and the entire New Testament was completed and printed in 1917, using Roman letters to represent the A-Hmao words. Samuel Clarke, who was also involved, summarized how the A-Hmao Bible gradually emerged:

> Compared with learning to read Chinese characters, it is very easy for them to read their own language phonetically, written in Roman letters. In May 1909, the first copies of Mark's Gospel arrived from the printer. Later on, the Gospel of Matthew was printed, and the Gospel of John, with his Epistles, is now in the hands of the printer . . .
>
> Soon the whole New Testament will be in the hands of the A-Hmao Christians. They are eager to learn to read, and those who can read are zealous in teaching others. Very soon they will be a reading community.[2]

At the same time, however, the genius missionary-linguist Samuel Pollard was pondering whether the A-Hmao might better understand God's Word by using a different orthography. While he was praying, he remembered reading about a unique script used to translate the Bible into the Native American Cree language.

After tweaking the Cree script to suit the tonal vernacular of the A-Hmao, Pollard began translating the Scriptures, hoping to make it as simple as possible for the uneducated tribespeople to learn. When the first portions became available, the believers were overjoyed. Because the new alphabet was so simple to learn, soon dozens of A-Hmao villages were holding Bible study classes. The Pollard script quickly gained favor among the A-Hmao Christians, and James Adam's Roman version soon fell into disuse.[3]

A sample of the Pollard script created for the A-Hmao people

Having the Bible added a great deal of dignity to the A-Hmao people, who were amazed that God had not forgotten them, and that He loved them so much as to have sent them His precious Book in their own language.

The A-Hmao were the first minority group in Guizhou to have the Scriptures in their language, and the Pollard script Bible is still widely used among them today. Alas, a century later, the A-Hmao remain one of only a small number of minority groups in all of China with the Word of God available in their own written language.

The Shui and other tribes

The Shui ethnic group in southern Guizhou was first visited by French Catholic missionaries in 1884, and by the early twentieth century there were some 5,000 Shui Catholics in 30 churches. An anti-Christian movement in 1906, however, resulted in many of the Shui church leaders being put to death, and the rest of the believers fell away.

Evangelical missionaries first contacted the Shui in 1910. A small group of Shui men heard that the missionaries were visiting Miao churches in the area and, eager to understand the Christian message, they sent delegates to meet the missionaries, who reported:

> A new interest has sprung up among the Shui . . . Hearing we had come, some of these men travelled overnight fearing we might have left before they met us. A few of these Shui were down at our Chinese New Year's conference. A son of the headman of that district is studying in our Anshun school this year . . . If the work is going to spread out in this way, the Lord will need to send more workers.[4]

Sadly, it appears that no new workers came to reach the Shui, and little mention was made of them in subsequent years and decades following this initial contact. Tragically, for nearly a hundred years few Shui people heard about Jesus Christ, and it was not until the twenty-first century that an effective church emerged among this gentle and friendly group, which today numbers approximately 500,000 people.

Although the missionaries were thrilled by the spiritual progress among several Miao groups, dozens of other neglected tribes lived scattered throughout the never-ending mountains and valleys of Guizhou. Some missionaries, having been trained to think rationally at seminaries in their home countries, were shocked by the spiritual darkness they encountered when they attempted to introduce the gospel to tribespeople for the first time.

William Hudspeth commented, "As a rule I don't believe in devils but these wizards seem to have great communications

*Four Christian women from a tribe known as the "Wooden Comb Miao"
near Anshun in 1914*

with a whole world of demons."[5] He went on to describe some
of the supernatural feats done by the spirit-priests, including
putting white-hot chains around their necks without being
harmed.

The Anshun missionaries came across several other tribes
during their frequent travels throughout Guizhou. One Miao
tribe they called the "Wooden Comb" or "Lopsided Comb"
Miao. This group lived about 20 miles (32 km) south of
Anshun, and were so named because of the women's elaborate
hairstyles. In 1914 Adam was thrilled to report:

> Two delegations from the Wooden Comb Miao came down the
> mountains asking for teachers to go and teach them the gospel.
> Peter and Timothy returned with them . . . They are now busy
> up in the mountains telling forth the old story of Jesus and His
> love . . .

> Travelling by another route, we came upon a new tribe called the Big-Horn Miao . . . We stopped, and spoke to them first in Chinese and then in one of our Miao dialects. They did not run away, but stood and listened to what I had to tell them . . . Oh when shall all the very long-waiting, lost tribes hear the message?
>
> Praise God for the many that are now hearing and learning the gospel. How the heart of the Lord Jesus Christ must rejoice over so many of His lost, wandering sheep finding their Good Shepherd at last.[6]

Adam visited another village just one month later, where he noted, "At this place Red-Turbaned, Water, and Wooden Comb Miao joined the meetings. The first-fruits from among the Wooden Comb Miao were baptized."[7]

The only doctor in Guizhou

In 1913 the population of Guizhou was estimated at between 12 and 18 million people, but not a single doctor worked in the entire province. Stirred by the reports of James Adam and others, a British doctor, Edward Fish, surrendered his life to God's service. Compelled by the love of Christ, Fish abandoned his financially lucrative career and relocated to the other side of the world to serve the impoverished people of Guizhou.

After gaining his orientation with the Adams in Anshun, in August 1913 Fish joined the intrepid missionary on one of his arduous journeys among the tribes. Having read the remarkable accounts of revival published in magazines, Fish had a romantic image in his mind of the work, but the harsh reality of what life was like in rural China soon struck him to the core of his being. The doctor wrote from one of the first villages they stopped at:

A boat with a party of Guizhou missionaries on board in 1913. At the time there were 31 missionaries in the province: 27 with the CIM and 4 Methodists

I arose early—about five o'clock—hoping to have a quiet time by myself before the duties of the day began. However, it was to be otherwise, for I had no sooner arisen than patients began to come and continued all day long. Only with the greatest difficulty was I able to get away for my meals. For over 12 hours I was just as busy as I could be. When I returned from dinner, they were lined up outside the door for a considerable distance, while the inside was packed with men, women, and children waiting for a chance to press their way up the ladder where I was at work. I must have seen nearly 400 patients.[8]

Although Dr. Fish's treatment was free to sick people, the generous-hearted Miao felt it wasn't right to receive treatment without giving something in return. At another village a few days later, Fish was excited when the first batch of mail from home caught up with him. He sat down on a bench intending to read his letters, but was soon completely surrounded by those in need. He wrote:

One man handed me a fowl, another came with a basket of eggs. This proved too much, and I arose and took my place where for three days I sought to minister to their needs. At this place I received over 500 eggs, 20 chickens, several pots of honey, baskets of potatoes, green corn, beans, etc.[9]

On one occasion, Fish was asked to visit a poor family in great need. He entered their dark and dingy hovel, and was scarcely able to see as he carefully made his way across the wet mud floor. All of a sudden he stepped on the foot of a small nine-year-old boy, who was lying naked with his back turned toward the fire. "It was most pathetic to see a child of such tender years lying on the damp mud floor in the grip of a disease. He strongly resisted every effort I made to examine him," wrote the stunned doctor, before his attention was attracted to another object. He recalled:

Turning back another ragged and filthy rug . . . I beheld a sight I believe I shall never forget. A woman lay there—dying. She, too, was lying on the damp ground, clad in the scant remnant of what was once a garment. Her hair was dishevelled, her form emaciated, both eyes glued together with a copious discharge, and her four limbs so entangled that I could scarcely find a place to put my stethoscope on her chest. She made no resistance. Once she tried to speak, but her strength was too far gone . . . The time of her departure was at hand . . .

All that passed through my mind at that time can better be imagined than described. Gazing upon the representatives of three generations, it seemed as though I never realized before what claims these people have upon me. How appalling their poverty! How great their need![10]

James Adam was a wise and loving man. He knew the new recruit was overwhelmed by his first journey, so when they returned to Anshun, Adam spent much time taking care of Fish and praying earnestly for him. Adam realized that treating the sick on long itinerant journeys was not the most productive way to utilize the doctor's skills. He decided to open a small hospital in Anshun, where people from throughout the region could come to be treated and receive medicine. When the hospital opened in 1914, Adam joyfully wrote:

> It is my great privilege to open the first hospital in this entire province . . . Great as the medical need is, it cannot be compared to the spiritual darkness—which is appalling. Our hospital and dispensary work must always ever be secondary in importance to the real needs of the people. While doing all that is within our power to alleviate their suffering and to heal their diseases, we must never forget that we are here, primarily, as ambassadors of our Lord Jesus Christ. May He give us the needed grace to be successful "fishers of men," and that when the day's work is done it may be "well done."[11]

James Adam oversaw the construction of the new CIM chapel at Anshun in 1915

Broken down with grief

Christian history is decorated with the lives of many outstanding missionaries. In Asia, individuals like William Carey, Adoniram Judson and Hudson Taylor inspired generations of believers, while David Livingstone of Africa became a household name. James Adam was much lesser known than those famous pioneers, but his sacrificial service for Jesus Christ stands tall in the annals of Christianity in Guizhou.

Adam had arrived in China in 1887, at the tender age of 23. He had served wholeheartedly for the next 28 years, and was preparing to travel home to Scotland on furlough when he was struck by a lightning bolt while standing on the porch of his home one evening in August 1915. The beloved missionary and one-time "King of the Miao" was dead at the age of 51.

Right up to the end of his time in this world, James Adam continued to preach the gospel to the lost and to baptize new believers into the family of God. His boundless joy and unquenchable passion for reaching the lost shone through in one of his final reports:

> This evening I baptized 126 men and 98 women; 224 trophies of the Lord's mighty saving power. Hallelujah! . . . The Lord's power and blessing were wonderfully manifested, and His love filled all our hearts. How greatly our Lord's own heart must have rejoiced tonight . . .
>
> It is like a bit of glory to hear 1,000 or more saved Miao singing with much vim . . . Think of it! These dear believers were once unrighteous, fornicators, demon worshippers, adulterers, unclean, drunkards, revilers, etc. . . . Oh, why do we ever limit the saving power of our God? All these Miao are saved, and washed to the glory of His great Name . . .
>
> Nearly all of the 626 children of God baptized have been true believers for at least one and a half years. Quite a large number hope to confess the Lord in baptism next time we visit.[12]

When the news of Adam's sudden death spread, a string of testimonials poured in from those who knew him best. John Stevenson, a leader of the CIM, wrote the following stirring tribute, which also revealed the size and influence that the Anshun mission had grown to encompass under Adam's leadership:

> A more indefatigable and hard-working missionary than Mr. Adam we have never had, a man who never spared himself and who was greatly beloved by those whom he was used to bring to the Lord . . .
>
> There have been baptized from the commencement in Anshun and district 6,449 people, and at the end of last year there were 5,590 communicants. When we think of the 42 evangelists, 29 school teachers, with 639 students and 323 unpaid helpers, one can realize a little of the magnitude of the work . . .
>
> No CIM worker has ever had the privilege of receiving so many converts into the visible Church, and I question whether any single missionary of any society has either . . . Now, just when he was about to take a much-needed furlough, he has suddenly been taken from us. Deepest sympathy is felt for his widow and two children in Scotland who had been looking for his return.[13]

Nearly a century after the death of James Adam, missiologists were still discussing the reasons behind his outstanding success. Ralph Covell commented:

> Untiring in travel to hundreds of villages, outgoing and friendly, fluent in the Miao language, he baptized nearly 7,000 of the Miao . . .
>
> Early in the work Adam sifted out those with potential for leadership and brought them into his own home for weeks of concentrated discipleship. Those initial disciples took the lead in preaching to and teaching the many hundreds who later would respond in this snowballing movement . . .

> Adam aggressively confronted Miao society with the claims of the gospel. After several people in a village were willing to confess the Name of Jesus publicly, Adam called for a bonfire, at which time all of the spirit paraphernalia was burned . . . Adam allowed no one to be baptized who had not made a clear break with the demon world.
>
> Even when only a few people in a village had believed, Adam, along with these converts, took the initiative in tearing down the houses used by the young people for their sexual orgies. He helped in sweeping out all remaining signs of idolatry, in cutting down spirit trees, and in finding and destroying all traces of opium, opium pipes, and lamps.[14]

Shockingly, Adam's death proved to be the first in a string of losses for the Church in Guizhou. Missionary Thomas Windsor had been chosen to replace Adam while he was away on furlough, but Windsor had only just arrived in Anshun and was settling in when he fell ill with dysentery and died.

The very next month (September 1915), Samuel Pollard also died after contracting typhoid fever at his mission station. Thus both of the pioneers who had worked so hard to reach the A-Hmao and to translate their Bible were suddenly taken away.

The following year even more sorrow came when Samuel Clarke, after 38 years in China, also went to be with the Lord. In a short space of time the Guizhou missionary community had lost four of its finest and most experienced leaders.

When the Miao and other Christians throughout Guizhou heard about Adam's death, many were distraught. The faith of some younger believers was shaken by the circumstances of his death, which caused them to question God's protection. The more mature church members quickly helped soothe their doubts, however, and shock at the news of Adam's passing soon turned to thanksgiving for a life well spent.

The final earthly word on James Adam's life fittingly went to two Miao Christians, who wrote a letter of sympathy to Adam's grieving widow in January 1916:

> Incalculably strange, that on the evening of the 29th day of the sixth moon, it was God's will to receive our beloved Pastor up to heaven, while we are left behind to mourn our loss.
>
> We were formerly dead in sin, passing our days in ignorance and darkness . . . The dear Pastor came bringing us the teaching of the Savior's love. He led thousands of us Miao to repent and believe in the Lord, and he loved us with a love surpassing the love of parents for their own children. Therefore, all the Miao believers were broken down with grief, just as though we had lost our own parents.
>
> Our hearts are pained beyond expression. We who are near cannot realize he has been taken from us to heaven. We cannot again serve him with our own hands, neither again will we hear his words of precious instruction . . .
>
> We deeply desire the speedy return of our Lord Jesus, then we shall again meet our beloved Pastor, and it is for this our hearts long . . .
>
> May the Triune God protect you and your family. Greetings to the two boys. We send this memorial to you with reverence.
>
> Yang Xiguang (Water Miao tribe)
>
> Tao Joshua (Flowery Miao tribe).[15]

A decade of growth

The initial years following the sudden loss of so many influential leaders were difficult ones for the Church in Guizhou. More than 10,000 A-Hmao Christians inhabited the areas of northwest Guizhou and adjacent parts of Yunnan when Adam and Pollard perished in 1915. The sudden removal of the duo struck the fledgling churches like a hammer blow, and in the next few years many who had placed their trust in the missionaries instead of Jesus Christ fell away from the faith. William Hudspeth noted, "After Pollard's death there was a recrudescence of drunkenness, immorality and superstition."[16]

The spiritual decay was exacerbated in 1918, when the worst famine in living memory struck the Stone Gateway area, leaving many A-Hmao feeling disenchanted toward God.

With the benefit of hindsight, however, the quality of the foundation laid by Adam and Pollard can be seen by the fact that more than a century after their deaths, approximately 80 percent of both the 400,000 A-Hmao (Big Flowery Miao) people and the 130,000 Gha-Mu (Small Flowery Miao) people continue to walk by faith in the Son of God.

Statistically, the Evangelical churches in Guizhou had experienced a decade of unprecedented growth. In 1904 the total number of Evangelical believers in the province was just 123, but by 1919 it had mushroomed to 20,873,[17] a number 170 times greater over the 15-year period.[18]

Catholics had also enjoyed significant growth in Guizhou, and they continued to enjoy numerical dominance over their Evangelical counterparts. In 1907 there had been a reported 25,368 believers in 106 Catholic churches throughout the province.[19] Fourteen years later in 1921, when the next reliable survey was conducted, the Catholics had grown to 35,286 members in 286 churches,[20] meaning there were nearly four times as many Catholics as Evangelicals in Guizhou at the time.

1920s

———•••———

Turmoil and strife

The 1920s was a distressing time not only for the Church in Guizhou, but for the population in general. The economy was in tatters due to hyperinflation, and a severe famine struck the province in the middle part of the decade, bringing unbearable misery upon the beleaguered people.

The tense atmosphere in China at the time created a leadership vacuum, which ultimately led to a long civil war between the Nationalists and the Communists. Guizhou had already been plunged into years of lawlessness and chaos before the full outbreak of hostility, with groups of bandits looting and murdering the terrorized population.

Because of the dire situation, churches in Guizhou did not enjoy the same numerical growth in the 1920s as they had enjoyed in the previous two decades. Times were stressful, and many Christians simply focused on surviving from one day to the next. At one location it was reported:

> The poor people have had a very trying year from swarming hordes of brigands. They had to band themselves together to fight off these invaders. Fortresses have been built all over the hills, from which they fought day and night battles. Many a time, whole villages of people spent the night, wet or dry, out on the hills for fear of attacks from robbers.[1]

The A-Hmao churches also adopted a defensive posture as they patiently waited for better times. In 1928, missionary Vaughan Rees sent out this prayer request after touring the region: "Pray for the A-Hmao. They are amidst trial and persecution and are struggling on alone, and have done so for some years, as there is no worker to send to them."[2]

The colporteurs

Because of the difficulties in traveling around the countryside in the 1920s, missionary activity was severely restricted in Guizhou. The gospel continued to go forth, however, through the courageous efforts of Christian "colporteurs" (a French word meaning "book peddlers").

These men often traveled through bandit-infested territory with large trunks full of Bibles, Gospels, tracts and other

Two A-Hmao Bible colporteurs in 1915

Christian books. They customarily set up stalls in marketplaces and villages, selling their literature at cost price to interested people. Despite the dangers, in 1927 one team of Miao colporteurs visited a hundred different villages, selling 8,000 books and 10,000 tracts.

Morris and Irma Slichter

The internal strife afflicting the people of China in the 1920s resulted in grave danger for foreign missionaries, but they faithfully continued to serve the Lord Jesus Christ. Morris and Irma Slichter and their children were based at the Anshun mission station. Despite the risks, Morris frequently traveled out to visit the tribal Christians. In 1926 he visited Dengdeng village, where a great number of Hmong Shua people had placed their trust in God when James Adam visited 20 years earlier. Slichter was overjoyed to report:

> There has been steady increase and adding to the Church, for which we praise God, for we know this can only be by His power . . . We reached there on a Friday evening, and as our coming had been announced, the Christians gathered all day Saturday from the country round about . . .
>
> Usually we hold a baptism service at this outstation once a year. On such occasions the candidates for baptism are examined by us along with the church elders from their own villages . . . This time at Dengdeng, 16 men and 14 women were accepted. The great majority of them were men with their wives, and mostly young people.[3]

After saying goodbye to the believers at Dengdeng, Slichter traveled to other villages in western Guizhou, baptizing small groups of converts at each place and encouraging the Christians by teaching God's Word. Before long, however, Slichter and his co-workers came across a group of bandits, "armed with daggers, swords, and rifles." They managed to evade trouble on that occasion, and the very next day they were met by a group of 30 to 40 Miao believers who came to escort them through more bandit-infested territory to their village. They learned that:

> Almost everybody had joined the robbers but the Christians, and the fact of their holding out made the robbers all the more incensed against them. One poor fellow had a huge scar on his upper lip where he had been slashed by the robbers. They cut his lip, they said, in order that he might not be able to give evidence against them . . . Our hearts go out to these poor people, for they are living in constant dread of the robbers. They dare not stay away from home after dark, nor sleep during the night.[4]

Despite the terrible conditions, Slichter and his assistants baptized another 58 new believers before commencing the next stage of their perilous journey. They survived by the providence of God, and were deeply relieved to return home to their families in Anshun.

The following May, 1927, Morris and Irma Slichter and their two small children (six-year-old John and three-year-old Ruth), accompanied by a single female missionary, Mary Craig, set out on a journey to Kunming, the capital city of Yunnan Province. After crossing the provincial border, the small party was set upon by a group of three murderous thieves. They attacked the missionaries:

> and heedless of their cry for mercy, one of them took aim and fired at Mrs. Slichter, who was holding little Ruth in her arms. The bullet struck the child in the head, and passing through, it tore an ugly gash in Mrs. Slichter's left wrist, as it fell to the ground. Another robber stabbed Morris Slichter in the back with his bayonet, evidently piercing his heart and killing him instantly. He fell without a sound.[5]

Incredibly, while the survivors lay on the ground injured and traumatized, another group of bandits came down the road and looted them of their remaining clothes and possessions, leaving them naked and destitute.

Irma Slichter, her son John, and Mary Craig somehow managed to survive, and finally made their way to Kunming. Heaven had gained two precious souls, but the gospel had suffered yet another setback in Guizhou.

The deliverance of little En Hui

Amid the chaos and violence that engulfed Guizhou in the 1920s, stories of deliverance emerged to bring cheer to the

En Hui with his father and grandfather

hearts of many Christians. One of the most touching stories involved a nine-year-old A-Hmao boy named En Hui, who was captured along with his grandfather in a raid by bandits on Kopu village in November 1928.

Grandfather Liu was allowed to return home with a ransom demand for little En Hui's life, but the boy was forced to march further into the mountains by the evildoers, along with a group of other hostages.

For months no news emerged about the captives, and En Hui's grandfather was distraught, blaming himself for not being able to protect his grandson. There was no way the impoverished family could afford to pay the ransom price. One day a letter arrived at Kopu, signed by En Hui himself. He said he was being treated badly, had contracted a skin disease, and that he would be killed if the ransom wasn't paid soon.

En Hui's grandfather was deeply troubled, and all the Christians at Kopu cried out to the living God day and night for deliverance. One day news suddenly arrived that the villagers' prayers were answered, and En Hui had been rescued!

Because he was too thin and weak to walk home, a sedan chair was arranged to collect En Hui and carry him back to Kopu. The A-Hmao Christians rejoiced greatly, and the whole community turned out to greet his arrival. A fattened pig was slaughtered and a great many guests were invited to the feast. En Hui's mother ran down the trail to welcome her son after five months in captivity. Meanwhile:

> Grandfather Liu had not gone out to meet En Hui, but waited at home to welcome him. The meeting was touching. He put his arms around the lad and clasped him, bowing his head in thanks to God for his deliverance. Then he just sat there, clasping the boy, quite overcome for a few minutes. A great load had rolled off the old man's shoulders, and he looked younger already . . .

Then the rejoicing and feasting began, people brought gifts, and gladness was on every hand. The father said, "I never thought I would be as happy as I am today. Thank God for delivering my soul." The lad himself said he knew it was an answer to prayer that he was free. He had been praying that soldiers might come and chase the brigands and thus set him free—and his prayers were truly answered.[6]

The most poorly occupied province in China

The internal conditions in Guizhou resulted in little progress for the gospel throughout the 1920s. Although encouraging signs were seen in some towns and among several minority groups, overall the Evangelical churches in the province had a defensive mindset, and much of their work was aimed at providing humanitarian relief for the suffering population, rather than proclaiming the gospel and planting churches.

Even the work among the A-Hmao, Gha-Mu and other Miao tribes, which had flourished in the previous two decades, entered a period of inertia where little growth occurred. Instead

The 1927 Guizhou CIM preachers' conference

101

of evangelism, more energy was spent on establishing believers in the faith. This strategy provided a stronger foundation for the tribal churches, and the benefits were to be seen in later decades.

Half a century after the first Evangelical missionaries arrived, the CIM had done a sterling job to the best of their God-given abilities, but Guizhou was unique among the provinces of China in that a single mission society almost completely dominated the work in an entire province, with only a handful of Methodist missionaries in northwest Guizhou adding variety to the mix.

Ironically, the tremendous revival among the A-Hmao and other tribes appears to have negatively affected the work in the rest of the province in two ways. First, other Evangelicals read the stirring accounts of thousands of baptisms and assumed the CIM was well placed to extend its work. Second, the CIM focused most of its missionaries and resources among those tribes, to the neglect of dozens of other unreached ethnic groups and the millions of Han Chinese in the province.

The lack of workers in a territory as large and populous as Guizhou was startling, with vast areas going without any gospel witness. The eastern and southern parts of the province were particularly neglected, to the point where a nationwide survey in 1922 expressed alarm at the lack of activity:

> Guizhou averages four missionaries per 1,000,000 inhabitants, and five per 1,000 communicants. When considered, therefore, solely from the standpoint of missionary occupation, Guizhou is the most poorly occupied province in China, the average for the entire country being almost four times better, or 15 missionaries per 1,000,000 population, and 19 per 1,000 communicants . . . Over one half of the province still remains unclaimed, although it is occasionally visited by colporteurs, Chinese evangelists, or missionaries.[7]

Although the reasons for such slow progress in the Guizhou missionary endeavor remain unclear, some reports suggest disunity and frustration, even among the two groups that were laboring in the province. The same survey noted:

> The United Methodist Church reports a meeting of its representatives with representatives of the CIM, at which the question of respective fields in western Guizhou was considered. The results of this meeting have not been satisfactory, and are, therefore, not acceptable to all concerned . . . Lack of funds, resulting in inadequacy of staff both foreign and native, is mentioned by all correspondents as the first and chief reason for the present inadequacy of Christian occupation.[8]

The contrast between Guizhou and neighboring provinces was stark. To the south in Guangxi—a province that shares many similarities—the first Evangelical missionaries arrived only in 1893, 16 years later than in Guizhou. The Christian and Missionary Alliance emerged as the prominent organization serving in Guangxi, but by the 1920s a dozen other mission societies were sharing the burden and helping spread the gospel. The CIM superintendent for Guizhou, Jack Robinson, lamented the lack of laborers in his province:

> We have in Guizhou working among the Chinese as distinct from the tribespeople, 44 foreign missionaries, and only 10 Chinese workers. That is, over four missionaries have to share one worker between them. In Guangxi, the Christian and Missionary Alliance have about 20 workers and about 140 Chinese helpers, or seven Chinese workers to each missionary . . . Thus for Guizhou to have the same ratio of Chinese workers to missionaries as they have in Guangxi we need 300 trained Chinese workers.[9]

The CIM was quick to oppose the Seventh-Day Adventists when they tried to gain a foothold in Guizhou. The CIM missionaries strongly disapproved of their doctrine and were

*Seventh-Day Adventist missionaries Claude and Irene Miller in A-Hmao
clothes, 1920s*

grieved by the spiritual condition of their members. Harry
Taylor wrote this scathing assessment from Guiyang:

> The Seventh-Day Adventists are few in numbers. In all places
> where there are members they are using money and influence
> to get believers to go to them, and for the last two or three years
> have been a disturbing influence in our district. They accept
> all excommunicated members and enquirers after the briefest
> instruction about keeping Saturday and not eating pork, and
> they give them status as church members. They then use their
> knowledge of the Christians to seek out all to entice them away.
> Their members smoke and deal in the soul-destroying opium,
> and are not rebuked for it.[10]

Whether the CIM workers consciously or subconsciously blocked other mission groups from operating in Guizhou is uncertain, but the harvest in most other Chinese provinces by this time was being gathered by numerous mission groups including Baptists, Presbyterians, Methodists, Pentecostals, Anglicans and others. In Guizhou, however, the CIM continued almost exclusively to dominate the Evangelical landscape.

The Catholics, on the other hand, had few restrictions on their work and their numbers increased sharply throughout the decade. In the early 1920s, Catholics in Guizhou outnumbered Evangelicals by almost a four-to-one ratio, and while many Evangelical churches were mired in a state of inertia, the Catholics surged ahead and nearly doubled their church membership by the end of the decade. Most of their work was concentrated in and around the capital city Guiyang, and in the southern districts of Guizhou.

1930s

A breakthrough among the Han

While the Christian world had rejoiced at the extraordinary revival among several tribes in Guizhou in the early twentieth century, most people were unaware that the millions of Han Chinese living throughout the province remained practically untouched by the gospel. In 1931—more than half a century after Broumton and Judd had first arrived in Guizhou—there were still entire counties that had never been visited by a missionary and where Jesus had yet to be named.

Unexpectedly, in 1931 a breakthrough of God's grace and power occurred among the Han Chinese at Dushan in southern Guizhou—the same town where two thousand families had prematurely expressed an interest in becoming

Christians at Bijie in 1938

Christians at the start of the century. The vessel chosen by the Holy Spirit to bring his blessing was a local pastor named Fang.

Over the Chinese New Year period a series of evangelistic meetings was held at Dushan. For three days the weather was fine and sunny (a rare occurrence in Guizhou), and between 150 and 200 people attended the meetings from throughout the area. Many people surrendered their lives to Christ, and a missionary said of Pastor Fang:

> I had almost despaired of seeing such a man in this province. He has been a Christian for 40 years and has gone on with the Lord. Although he has been through much trouble, he is such a happy man. He keeps true to the Scriptures.[1]

Fruit at Weng'an

Harry Taylor of the CIM had been based at Guiyang since 1927. Work in the provincial capital had proven difficult, with few people showing any interest in the message of eternal life. Taylor was encouraged by news of the breakthrough at Dushan, and decided to visit the nearby Weng'an area to see if there would be a similar response to the gospel. After traveling to the south of the province with a Chinese co-worker and a large supply of Christian literature, Taylor was shocked to find a spiritual hunger among the people such as he had never seen in Guiyang. He shared:

> As it was market day when we arrived we soon had a crowd of interested people besieging us. The evangelist was preaching and selling gospels at the front door of an inn during the afternoon, and I had a good time preaching to the crowd of about 200 that listened very attentively . . .
>
> Afterward we learned that an old sorcerer over 60 years of age heard us that day and believed. He came in more than once

to ask about the gospel and said he realized that he would have to start a new life and give up his sins . . .

After about eight days we began to see fruit, and a shopkeeper, whose business was to sell paper connected with idolatry, came to see me and said that he wanted to believe. I explained the way of salvation, and got him on his knees praying and confessing his sins. So we did with all who claimed to be real. This man was willing to burn his stock of paper, with the idol on the top of it. His action and subsequent witness made a profound impression on the city.

Then came another who had a small stall on the street and he also took a definite stand. These two made a practice of coming each evening for Bible study and prayer. Then they brought others who were interested and we dealt with them.[2]

Finally, after many generations of people had gone into a Christless eternity without hearing the gospel, this one visit resulted in the formation of the first Evangelical church in the history of Weng'an. Several months later it was reported:

Altogether we have the names of almost 20 men and women who were dealt with at Weng'an, and many more are interested. At the beginning we prayed that as a result of our visit there should be a church in the city when we left. God has answered.[3]

Most of the missionaries up to that point believed that the most effective strategy was to reach the largest cities first, and that the gospel would automatically radiate out to other districts. The problem was that the churches in Guiyang had never been beacons of light, but were filled with many problems and weaknesses. Buoyed by the success of his trip to Weng'an, Taylor encouraged other missionaries in the capital also to visit outlying districts, and the fame of Jesus gradually spread to many parts of the province for the first time.

The tide turns in Guizhou

The 1930s saw strong Christian growth in many parts of China, as the Holy Spirit visited His people with great power. Revival came to many churches, but remote Guizhou Province remained largely unaffected, until the Bethel Band Mission visited the Anshun area in 1934. Before the meetings commenced, six weeks of fervent intercession took place. Consequently, when the preaching got underway:

> A startling movement began, one in which the confession of awful sins preceded the revival of believers and the salvation of non-Christian tribespeople. Late in 1935, the revival was continuing among the Miao tribes and a profound work of grace was going on at Anshun. The revived Christians formed many preaching bands which went everywhere preaching the Word . . .
>
> More than six months later, the missionaries were still telling of prayer meetings going on till midnight, with a deep sense of

This multi-ethnic band of evangelists toured Guizhou in the mid-1930s. The members included two Han, two Miao, and one Nosu preacher

conviction followed by a manifestation of confession and crying for forgiveness.[4]

The effect of the ministry by the Bethel Bands was far-reaching. Many of the foreign missionaries in Guizhou had labored for years with little success, and the fresh wave of the Holy Spirit was like rain on a parched and thirsty land. Missionary Eugene Crapuchettes attended the meetings in Anshun and was deeply touched. He reported:

> The Spirit worked mightily and there was loud crying and seeking acceptance with God . . . A young fellow cried out for his relatives, being greatly pressed in the Spirit, fearing lest they fall into hell. He later went to them and pleaded with them to come to the meeting, but only received rebuffs. He could not contain himself and cried before them. Strangely enough, they were building a house and two of the largest beams broke in the middle—no one knows how—and the combination of circumstances induced them to go. They were blessed, too.[5]

In Zunyi—a strategic town whose name means "to observe righteousness"—missionary Charles Chapman had labored for several years with little outward sign of progress until the revival touched the believers there. Chapman testified:

> I have been itinerating with the Evangelistic Band for some eight weeks, during which many hundreds of tracts were scattered, gospel portions and New Testaments sold and posters used. The Lord was with us and we have had much joy in the proclamation of His Word. Indeed, I have never had such a time with the Chinese brethren before.
>
> Praise God, we believe that the tide has turned for blessing in Guizhou—there is a different spirit abroad, in the Church, among the workers, in witnessing on the street. Everything seems different. Much more prayer is being made by the Chinese themselves, and we are hoping and praying that this year's Bible school will result in a mighty strengthening of

A Christian family at Zunyi in 1933

those whom we believe the Lord will use in the reviving of His work.[6]

The Spirit of God searched people's hearts at a village called Bei Madong, and many were placed under intense conviction, causing them to cry out to Jesus Christ for relief. As a result, a missionary wrote:

> Confession of most awful sins took place, many times in the presence of those who had been offended. What greatly rejoiced my heart was to see a Hmong Shua (a most numerous tribe and very difficult to reach, and among whom are only a few cold Christians) break down in a most pitiable condition. I thought his heart would break as he confessed most terrible sins and it was some time before he received peace.

The students and faculty of Guizhou Bible School in 1936

Many of these people were cold and unyielding until the break came, but afterwards were as humble and gentle as children. A notable case was a young man whose brother was first blessed. He insisted he had no sin and was perfectly all right, but in one of the meetings, although it was a freezing cold day, his face was running with perspiration, and he looked as though someone had thrust a dagger into his heart. Later he received joy.[7]

The impact of the visitation of God's Spirit among the Guizhou churches in 1934 and 1935 was immediate and powerful. A new sense of unity and love was manifested between believers who had previously been cold toward one another. Many Christian students were revived and transformed, and Guizhou Bible School received an influx of new students eager to study God's Word in preparation for service.

The Ge

The Ge are one of dozens of distinct people groups inhabiting the hills of eastern Guizhou. Numbering more than 130,000 people today, the Ge have been included in the huge and diverse Miao nationality by the Chinese government, but they consider themselves distinct from the Miao and they proudly possess their own history, customs and language.

After the energetic Australian missionary Maurice Hutton completed his translation of the Hmu New Testament in 1934, his focus shifted to the nearby Ge tribe. The following year he remarked:

> The best and most cheering news of all to us is that one of the newly baptized believers is a Ge tribesman. It reminds me of the

A Ge girl in traditional dress
Paul Hattaway

nine years of prayer and work to get an entrance into that tribe and the one soul—now there are six men and I hear their wives and families are interested in the gospel too . . . The Lord has been burdening my heart for these Ge tribespeople without any portion of God's Word in their language.[8]

In 1937 Hutton reported that "Several Ge families have believed and we are at present having the Gospels of Mark and John and a catechism and some hymns and choruses printed, for we have also reduced their language to writing for them."[9]

Hutton used the same phonetic script to translate the Ge Scriptures as he had done with the Hmu New Testament. Although the Ge books were printed, no evidence exists that they were ever sent to the area or distributed among the Ge.

Tragically, in the early 1950s it appears the Ge Christians gave up their faith when the missionaries were expelled from China. One observer bluntly noted, "They believed in the missionaries and not in Jesus."[10]

Several decades passed before a small Ge church once again emerged in the 1990s. Today there are believed to be only about a hundred believers among this little-known tribe.

Five hundred and sixty days in captivity

The Guizhou town of Zunyi is revered in China for being the first major stop during the famous Long March of the Communist army. The revolutionaries commenced their epic journey with 85,000 men and women, but by the time they entered Zunyi a few months later they had only 30,000 troops left. A special meeting was held in the town, at which Mao Zedong emerged as the new leader of the Chinese Communist Party and the commander of the Red Army.

The lives of two CIM workers were dramatically altered by the Long March. On October 1, 1934, Rudolf Bosshardt, from

Rudolf Bosshardt before being taken hostage (left); and after his release 80 weeks later (right)

Switzerland, and New Zealander Arnolis Hayman were captured by the Sixth Red Army near Jiuzhou in the Hmu tribal area. The missionaries thought they would be quickly released, but in December they were put on trial by the Communists after a failed attempt to escape. Among the charges leveled against the pair were:

> The two prisoners by means of the Bible drugged the masses and brought them under their control . . . The said prisoners have learnt the Miao language and have deeply entered into the caves of these people. In Jiuzhou of those who have been deceived and joined the Church, 90 percent are of the Miao tribe.[11]

The men were told they were deserving of death, but instead, they were moved around the countryside by the Communists as ransom demands were made to their families and the mission. For many months the wives of the two hostages endured an emotional rollercoaster, as false reports of their deaths were received. The ransom demands started at $100,000 each, but when payment was not forthcoming the amounts increased.

Meanwhile, news of the kidnapped missionaries spread throughout the Christian world, and thousands of believers were interceding for the men and their heartbroken families.

As their captors' patience began to wear thin, Bosshardt and Hayman were beaten with bamboo canes. For months they were forced to march across mountains and through remote areas of four different provinces. The dire conditions took a heavy toll on the men, who were often accompanied by other hostages, including a French Catholic priest.

Some of the Chinese hostages whose families were unable to pay the ransom were executed by the cruel and heartless Communists. One poor woman, who was unable to keep up, was unanimously voted to be killed. Bosshardt recalled that the executioner was a young man about 20 years old, who "borrowed a sharp sword and dragged her away, followed by a second comrade carrying a hoe. Soon they returned smiling, and as indifferent as though they had done nothing more than kill a chicken for dinner."[12]

The CIM, meanwhile, had raised funds in a bid to pay the ransom, but communicating with the Communists proved difficult, as they were constantly on the move. When money was finally handed over, the Communist judge sneered at the men and deceitfully told them that only half of the payment had been met, so they could release only one of the hostages. Because he was older, Hayman was released and allowed to return to his family after 413 days in captivity.

Now alone with the Red Army, Bosshardt did all he could to focus on the Lord Jesus Christ, and he continued to share his faith with the soldiers. On one occasion he was surprised when the general tried to mock Bosshardt by telling the company, "He believes the Lord Jesus shall come a second time and call the faithful to Himself. When this happens and all the good people are gone, then the Communists will be able to put through their program."[13]

Many more months went by, as the soldiers and their prey doubled back by marching hundreds of miles through muddy and leech-infested regions of Guizhou, until they passed into Yunnan Province. The Nationalists were stronger in Yunnan, and the Communists decided to abandon the missionary and move on without him. Ironically, one of the most dangerous moments in the entire ordeal came after Bosshardt was released. Seeing him clothed in filthy rags and with a long unkempt beard, the Nationalist soldiers believed he was a Russian Communist spy and were preparing to kill him when they discovered his true identity.

On Easter Monday, 1936, Bosshardt was placed on a horse, and rode the last stage into Kunming. As he approached the city, three missionaries rode toward him. When they saw it was their missing colleague, the men burst into singing the doxology. One of them said:

> He looked so pale, ill and emaciated, but he was so cheerful . . .
> He was too weak even to ride a horse. His legs were swollen, and he had been wearing the clothes he had on for four months without having changed once . . . His hair and beard badly needed the barber's attention. The joy of holding his hand and welcoming him back among us will not soon be forgotten . . .

Bosshardt was brought in a rickshaw to the home of a missionary, where a warm bath, clean clothes and bed awaited him. A bonfire disposed of the Chinese clothes he had been

The first pictures of Hayman (left) and Bosshardt (right) after 413 and 560 days in captivity

wearing, and all accumulated attachments. The sensation of being clean, comfortable and shaven for the first time in many weary months can only be fully appreciated by those who have had a like experience.[14]

After such a long and harrowing ordeal, God's hand continued to be upon Bosshardt and Hayman, and the difficult experience didn't appear to impact their lives negatively. Arnolis Hayman lived a full life until his death in Sydney, Australia, at the age of 81, while Rudolf Bosshardt shocked many by returning to serve God in Guizhou until he and his wife Rose were expelled by the Communists in 1951.

1940s

The Church in decay

During the 1940s, the Church in Guizhou experienced what one mission journal described as:

> a very serious process of retrogression and decay, which if not soon arrested will, in many a tribal district which in the past has been the focus of prayers and the scene of victories in the Lord's Name, bring us back to our starting point again.[1]

In response to the need, a Bible school was established in the town of Gebu, south of Anshun. The school continued to function until the onset of Communism in 1949. With an average of 30 to 40 students each year, the school helped address the spiritual decay of many of the minority churches at the time. Rowland Butler, a missionary associated with the school, wrote:

> During the years that followed the advance of the Communist forces (1934–1936), the tribal Christians were left to their own leadership for long periods. Being an emotional people, and possessing only the New Testament and a small hymn-book in their own language, few of them being able to read, and fewer able to understand what they read, erroneous teaching crept in, which threatened the undoing of the whole Church. The local missionaries decided the only remedy lay in a Bible school for all the evangelists and teachers.[2]

The Anshun region had long been a strategic hub for numerous people groups in Guizhou. From the time that James Adam was first based there in the late 1890s, Anshun had been a vibrant center for Christianity in the province, and thousands of baptisms had been conducted in the city.

When Leslie Lyall—a CIM worker and author—moved to Anshun from northern China in 1941, however, he was dismayed to find that the spiritual light of the Church in the city had dimmed to little more than a flicker. By 1943, Lyall described the once flourishing church in Anshun as "almost non-existent." He wrote:

> We have been in Anshun for just over two years. The conditions in this province are in contrast to the flourishing churches in north China. Among the poor and despised tribes the response to the gospel has been very large, but among the Chinese it has been very small indeed . . . Though the church in Anshun is almost non-existent . . . we long to see men coming under the mighty conviction and quickening of the Holy Spirit. Nothing less will serve in a heathen land to turn men away from their superstitions, their materialism and above all, their sins.[3]

Thankfully, the backsliding of the Anshun Christians did not continue, and just a few years later it was noted, "Only a handful of Christians remained; the church was dead. Last year, however, the big chapel was filled for the Sunday services, and the church supported its own pastor."[4]

The Friedenshort Deaconess Mission

One of the more interesting and effective Evangelical mission organizations to work in Guizhou was the Friedenshort Deaconess Mission, which was founded in the Upper Silesia region of the German empire. Although the sisters in the mission sometimes dressed like Catholic nuns, they were an overtly Evangelical group that courageously served in Guizhou for decades, until their mission was finally shut down by the Communists in the 1940s.

The mission was established after its founder, Eva von Tiele-Winckler, met Hudson Taylor when he visited Switzerland. Eva

Eva von Tiele-Winckler

later attended the Keswick Convention in England, where she received a call from God to help serve the poor in China.

The first sister was sent to Hong Kong in 1905, but when four women volunteered to work among the tribes of Guizhou, the CIM accepted the Friedenshort Mission as an associate member. From the start, the women were effective servants of the gospel, pioneering medical and children's work among the impoverished tribes.

During the First World War all funding from Germany was cut off, but the sisters persevered at their isolated base near Dafang in northwest Guizhou. Their headquarters were situated 6,000 feet (1,830 meters) above sea level in a village that was often cut off by snow during winter. Their location was so remote that even the leaders of the mission usually traveled out of the region only once a year to attend the CIM conference, and to collect mail and supplies.

Ruth and Hannah Chen

The Friedenshort Mission was greatly appreciated by the local tribespeople, and the work received a boost when two Chinese sisters, Ruth and Hannah Chen, joined the mission. A 1933 report by the leader of the mission at the time, Sister M. C. Welzel, provided an insight into why its members were so effective in reaching various ethnic groups for Christ despite years of overwhelming difficulty:

> Besides the work among different Miao tribes in the district, such as the A-Hmao, Gha-Mu, Hmong Shua, Hmong Daw and Wooden Comb Miao, a movement began among the Nosu, so that for several years we were hardly able to respond to all the calls and also teach the converts . . .
>
> In the midst of this happy work, we experienced years of famine, accompanied by epidemics of various fevers, the result being a high death-rate. We also lost two sisters from typhus.

Whole villages died out because of this dreaded disease, and also for want of food, and many people moved to lower areas, most of whom never returned . . . Cruel persecutions of believers have been frequent.

Still the work went on, though much hindered, and hundreds of converts were gathered in. In 1925 . . . work began in the city of Bijie, a long day's journey to the northwest of Dafang . . . We are glad to say that the number of workers has gradually increased. Two Miao pastors and a number of Nosu and Miao helpers and elders, school teachers and Biblewomen, as well as a few Chinese helpers, are sharing the burden of the work and taking more responsibility . . .

The work among the Chinese has been more difficult, and they usually keep aloof from the tribes and Nosu, whom they despise. Still, a number have also been won to the Lord's side. Not a few have been won through dispensary work, for this is also an appalling need, as the nearest doctors and hospitals are many days' journey away. Then there is the need of the many lepers throughout the district. Work among them has just started.[5]

Saving the lepers

With China in turmoil because of civil war, the Friedenshort sisters continued to reach out to the many lepers who lived in the mountains. Sister Welzel reported:

The Lord opened a door for the almost untouched Nosu, who live in large numbers in western Guizhou . . . Some of our best evangelists and Christians are from among these people. Ordinarily the Chinese, Nosu and Miao have little intercourse, the former despising the latter; but in Christ the wall of partition is broken down. Our workers are from all three classes and work together in love and harmony. Among our lepers are Chinese, Nosu, Miao and Hmu.[6]

A group of lepers who surrendered their lives to Jesus Christ

After decades of grim struggle in the barren mountains, the Friedenshort Mission faced its most severe trial when the Communist army swept through its area. The leader of the work in Bijie at the time was an A-Hmao pastor named Paul Chang, who later summarized his experiences:

> I sometimes thought that I had never suffered for my Lord, but in February 1936 the Reds came to Bijie. Many left the city, but I felt it was my duty to stay and help the Christians in time of need. When the Reds heard that I was the pastor of the church they captured me and I had to pass through many trials at the hands of these evil men. But I had wonderful experiences too, for the Lord was near me.
>
> They beat me badly and burned my face, but while doing so the ravens came making a great noise. The Reds superstitiously

took this as a bad omen and set me free. The Lord used the ravens to save me, praise His wonderful Name! . . .

Those experiences helped me to come nearer to the Lord, to love my Bible more, and to pray more, and to be eager to do the Lord's work. Formerly I read through the Bible once a year, now I read it through at least three times a year.[7]

As conditions deteriorated, Ruth Chen managed to send out a letter, explaining how:

she and two of the lady teachers and two evangelists were on the hills for 19 nights and days, often having to walk all night in the dark and spending whole days without food. While hiding they could see the Reds and hear them offering farmers $500 for every foreigner that was taken. The mission compound was robbed, and doors and furniture burnt.[8]

The tumultuous experiences of the Friedenshort sisters at the hands of the Chinese Communists were mirrored back in Europe, where their home region became part of Communist East Germany, before being incorporated into Poland. During the chaos that engulfed Europe, the archives of the mission were destroyed. As a result, little is known about what happened during its final years, or what became of believers like Paul Chang and the Chen sisters.

In northwest Guizhou, however, the effects of the work of these courageous and faith-filled women have endured. Today many Nosu, A-Hmao and other Christians inhabit the desolate mountain communities near Dafang and Bijie. The work of the little-known Friedenshort Deaconess Mission greatly contributed to the rich Christian heritage in this part of Guizhou.

The shining A-Hmao Church

For decades the A-Hmao churches had steadily grown in grace, while experiencing many setbacks along the way. Missionaries

William and Muriel Rae, who served among the A-Hmao in the late 1930s and early 1940s, told how the Christians received a God-given strategy to share the gospel with unbelievers. This new approach provided a great boost to the work.

For centuries the widespread A-Hmao communities had gathered once or twice a year at large festivals, where the people offered sacrifices to placate the evil spirits. Tens of thousands of A-Hmao people attended the festivals, which afforded an opportunity for people to catch up with relatives and friends, while youngsters looked for potential suitors.

After attending one of the major A-Hmao festivals, Muriel Rae wrote, "Musicians played bamboo pipes ranging in length from three to 12 feet, which played in unison produced frightfully discordant sounds thought to dispel the spirits."[9] The bamboo pipes Rae referred to are called *lusheng*, and are used

Miao playing traditional lusheng *pipes in Guizhou*
Miao Messenger

by many Miao tribes and by other minority groups in south China.

For decades the A-Hmao Christians had not attended these festivals, for they no longer feared demons nor had a need to appease them. Their absence created tension between believers and their unsaved relatives. The A-Hmao Christians realized they needed to start attending the festivals again, and they viewed them as opportunities to spread the fame of Jesus Christ. William Rae remarked:

These popular events are tremendous opportunities for the A-Hmao to mingle with their kinsfolk—to tell them of their own marvelous deliverance from fear . . . As music resounded in the hills, the Christians moved about in the crowd, their gentle, mild manner and glowing faces attracting attention from those who wondered about the radical change in their demeanor. The Christians were quick to explain how they, too, had once been

Three A-Hmao Christian women

fearful and in bondage, but had been introduced to One who could set them free. The Christians promised to visit villages to teach them this "better way".[10]

The decision by the A-Hmao Christians to attend the festivals made a huge impact, as believers reconnected with the rest of their tribe and the gospel was shared. The churches began to grow again, and thousands of new A-Hmao believers entered the kingdom of God. When a missionary visited the remote A-Hmao base at Kopu in 1945 he reported:

> Hundreds of baptisms are still taking place, and the church membership is about 4,000, while maybe half of that tribe may be reckoned as under Christian influences . . . Never shall I forget the thrill of preaching at their annual convention. There were 1,300 crowded into the huge chapel for the noon service on the Sunday, and most of these stayed for the Communion service which followed. These hill-folk are grand singers; hymn-singing in four parts was a real inspiration.[11]

A changing of the guard

In May 1949 it was apparent that all of China would soon fall under Communist control. The British consul general ordered UK citizens to leave China, and as most of the missionaries among the A-Hmao were British, they evacuated their posts. One of the departing missionaries wrote:

> I was absolutely amazed at how quickly the Church recovered from the bewilderment which came with the Consul's order. The A-Hmao leaders at Stone Gateway immediately started planning for the future. We were running very short of copies of the hymnbook in the Pollard script, and being afraid that when the Communists arrived the printing of all Christian literature would be banned, the A-Hmao set up and duplicated several hundred copies.[12]

A-Hmao Christians on a hillside at Kopu in 1948

The printing was completely paid for by the local believers, and a special service was held where "the two themes were praise and thankfulness for the past, and a full realization that the Church was now theirs and their responsibility."[13]

As the final missionary left the area, a respected A-Hmao church leader named Zhu Huanzhang told P. K. Parsons:

> Teacher, when you get to England, please thank all the friends for their continued powerful support. We do not know what will happen when the Communists come. It may be that we will not be permitted to run our schools and our churches, but do not be afraid. The truth of God is deep in our hearts and can never be taken from us.[14]

The A-Hmao had possessed the New Testament in their language since 1917. In the 1940s plans were made to translate the Old Testament, but the arrival of Communism postponed the work. Another 60 years were to pass until 2009, when the more than 200,000 A-Hmao Christians in China finally had the entire Bible available in their language.

For the Church in Guizhou, the 1940s concluded in much the same way as previous decades—the A-Hmao and a few other tribes in western Guizhou had thriving churches, while the rest of the province remained largely unevangelized.

One study of the Church in Guizhou just prior to Communist rule in 1949 found there were 100,000 Evangelical Christians in the province.[15] This number represented almost a fivefold increase in the three decades since a 1922 study listed just 20,873 Evangelicals in Guizhou.[16]

The Catholics, on the other hand, had struggled to advance. By 1950 their numbers had scarcely increased in three decades, with a total of 41,813 church members reported throughout the province.[17]

The Nosu

The Nosu people are thought to have lived in the rugged mountains of western Guizhou for at least two thousand years. Their origins are uncertain, but their language places them as part of the great Tibeto-Burman race. Like many other native peoples in China and around the world, the Nosu possess an ancient flood legend, which has been passed down for countless generations. The Nosu account says:

> A certain man had three sons. He received warning that a flood was about to come upon the earth, and the family discussed how they should save themselves when this calamity came upon them. One suggested an iron cupboard, another a stone one, but the suggestion that they should make a cupboard of wood and store it with food was acted upon.[1]

A group of Nosu Christian women in 1914

131

Although today they are considered just one part of the multifaceted and artificial "Yi" minority group created by the Chinese government, for centuries the Nosu people in western Guizhou and neighboring provinces were renowned for their fierce independence. The Han commonly called them derogatory names, and even after the Chinese empire had expanded its influence, the terrified Chinese generally refused to enter Nosu territory, which they considered off limits.

Missionary Samuel Pollard described some of the conflicts between the Chinese and the Nosu:

> After a fight, the warriors who are killed on either side are opened up and their hearts removed, perhaps also their tongues, and these are cooked and eaten. It is supposed to be a way of inheriting the courage and valor of the deceased.[2]

For many generations the Nosu captured slaves, and did not discriminate between races. They took Chinese slaves, forced thousands of Miao and other tribespeople to serve them, and didn't hesitate even to take other Nosu captive to work their fields. During the Second World War, some of the British and American pilots who flew supplies from Burma into China were forced to parachute out of their airplanes over the Nosu region and were never heard from again. Rumors spread that they too had been taken into slavery by the Nosu who dwell in the nearly impenetrable Daliangshan ("Great Cold Mountains") in neighboring Sichuan Province.

While Nosu areas in Sichuan were considered too dangerous to visit until recent decades, the government was able to subdue the Nosu in Guizhou more easily. In 1727 the emperor Yang Cheng sent troops into the Nosu areas and slaughtered tens of thousands of people. As a result, great numbers of Nosu migrated away from their traditional homeland.

Conditions among the Nosu were reportedly so dire and unhygienic in the 1900s that their very survival was questioned. One writer noted:

> The unsanitary conditions in which they live—the water they drink is often drawn from stagnant pools fouled by sheep and cattle—and their riotous indulgence in whisky, opium, and other vices, sufficiently account for this . . . They are burdened with the thought that their doom as a race is sealed.[3]

Although Christianity among the A-Hmao and other Miao tribes had flourished in Guizhou since the early twentieth century, the gospel had barely touched the more than 70 other people groups scattered throughout the province.

Divisions of Nosu

The Nosu were traditionally divided into two main classes of people. "Black Nosu" were the slave owners who possessed

A Nosu Christian woman

vast tracts of land in west and northwest Guizhou and across the borders in Sichuan and Yunnan. The "White Nosu" were the serf class with no rights whatsoever. For centuries they were enslaved and mistreated by the Black Nosu. Some were forced into slavery because of debt and economic necessity, but many others were captured by fearsome raiding parties. Sweeping into villages on horseback, the Black Nosu looted and burned communities to the ground, taking away whomever they wished. The plight of the slaves was pitiable. Most were chained up and forced to work like pack animals, and many quickly perished.

The Nosu penchant for taking people by force also manifested itself in the notorious tradition of "bride snatching," when groups of Nosu men descended on a village and carried off a pretty girl, who would be forced to marry one of their number. The grieving parents would often never see the girl again, leaving them heartbroken for the rest of their lives.

There are four main Nosu groups in Guizhou today, each speaking its own language. The largest group, numbering more than 200,000 people, has been labeled the Panxian Nosu after the county they predominantly occupy. The three other Nosu groups in Guizhou are the Wusa Nosu, the Shuixi Nosu, and a small subgroup of about 5,000 Tushu people, who are the descendants of slaves.

After the fire of the gospel blazed through A-Hmao communities in the early 1900s, the attention of some missionaries turned to the Nosu further north. Unsurprisingly, the White Nosu slaves were far more receptive to the offer of salvation, while the Black Nosu slave owners were resistant. They were concerned that a shift to Christianity would usurp their dominance over the people of the region.

When the missionaries began to reach out to the Nosu with the gospel they met stiff opposition. Samuel Pollard wrote in 1905:

We crossed the sides of a big mountain . . . and finally arrived at the fort of a Nosu landlord called Loh-chig. He received us kindly and we stayed there the night . . . He told us straight he would rather lose his head than become a Christian. He refused all gifts of books, disputed all we said, and denied all our attempts to win him over. He stuck up strongly for his religion and defended the worship of idols with great zest.[4]

Undeterred, Pollard and his colleagues continued to sow the seed of the gospel. The fire of the Holy Spirit began to burn among the Nosu living on the Yunnan side of the border, and soon spread to Weining County in Guizhou.

By 1907, not only had White Nosu slaves turned to Christ, but even some Black Nosu had bowed their knees to the King of Kings. Pollard rejoiced:

A blind Nosu here who has become a Christian has released all his slaves and burnt the papers that bound them to him. He told them that they could remain as tenants. He has persuaded his nephew to do the same and other families have followed suit. Some he has persuaded to destroy their idols.[5]

It was Pollard who first suggested that where Miao and Nosu people lived alongside each other, the believers should meet together on Sundays and worship in whatever language was common to each group. The two peoples had long kept their distance, but now the love of Jesus Christ was breaking down the dividing walls of hostility and a remnant of redeemed Nosu people was emerging. In a diary entry dated July 2, 1910, Pollard noted, "Today I saw a miracle. At this lonely place the church was full of Nosu, and at their request Chang Yuehan (John Chang) was preaching to them. The proud Nosu listened to one of their Miao serfs."[6]

Although James Adam's work had focused on the A-Hmao and other Miao tribes, in 1911 he also wrote about his first

A White Nosu evangelist

Nosu converts. After a journey through northwest Guizhou, Adam reported:

> We rejoiced to see the way in which the gospel is taking hold of the poor despised White Nosu (who are mostly slaves). There is a fine work of grace going on among this class of Nosu. I specifically ask prayer for them. They are all exceedingly poor, but oh, so very earnest in learning the gospel. A dear White Nosu man named Joseph is the leader, and the Lord's chosen vessel for pouring blessing upon the very lowly folk. He knows the Scriptures well, and is always ready to answer the questions put by the preacher in the meetings. The Master has blessed our brother and is making him a big blessing to others.[7]

A group of Nosu men followed Adam back to his home in Anshun, so that they could learn more about Christianity. The hope, as with the A-Hmao several years earlier, was that these earnest seekers would return home as born-again Christians, becoming the vessels for the gospel to reach thousands of their fellow tribesmen and women.

In the following years a significant number of White Nosu did become followers of Jesus, but the Black Nosu rose up in opposition and put some of the new believers to death. James Adam realized that as long as the new believers remained enslaved, the Christian faith would struggle to survive among them. After prayer, he came up with a strategy to help the White Nosu and Miao Christians purchase small plots of land from their Black Nosu oppressors. This altered the course of the believers' lives. Adam listed the benefits of this initiative:

> No more paying of exorbitant rents. No more going off in daily gangs to work the chieftain's lands without receiving either pay for work done, or food while laboring for a cruel, hard landlord. No more paying of silver, or having animals taken whenever the landlord fancied he required use of both. No more imprisonments in dark dungeons, with heavy chains weighing the sufferers down, because the wicked landlord could find neither the needed silver nor the coveted animals in the poor tenant's home.[8]

The gospel takes root

When missionary Isaac Page moved into the Nosu area, he employed a dual strategy of reaching both the Nosu and their Miao neighbors. Page was encouraged by the progress and reported in 1918:

> The work is opening up on all sides, among both Miao and Nosu. Crowds of the latter are coming to enquire, and we thank God who enabled us to make our home among these tribes-people. Any inconvenience that living in such a wild place entails soon drops out of sight when we see souls pressing into the kingdom. In all, 134 have been received into the church at this time, and many more are hoping to be so.[9]

Chiopa, a Black Nosu church leader

In the early 1920s, a mission survey rejoiced at the progress that was taking place among the Nosu people. In describing how many had come to faith in the living God, the report noted:

> The Holy Spirit has given gifts to the Church in Guizhou even as He did in the early days. These men, with little education, have proved themselves equal to the task, and the Church has been built up in a very real way . . . Every Christian is a potential evangelist, and the tribespeople, almost everywhere, do all the evangelizing, the missionary following in their wake to consolidate what has been done . . .
>
> During the last year more than 1,000 families have come to us as enquirers, nearly all of whom belong to the White Nosu, or Tushu. Their interest in the gospel had been awakened through a number of our voluntary helpers, as well as through the work of our A-Hmao evangelists.

One man of this Tushu tribe—a farmer and who does Christian work voluntarily—is arranging to visit all the villages of his people where there has been any interest manifested, and intends to spend three days in each place and give what help he can to these new enquirers.[10]

The work among the Nosu continued to expand, and many people repented of their sins and put their trust in Jesus as the gospel spread from village to village throughout the rugged hills and deep valleys of northwest Guizhou.

In His wisdom, God primarily chose the Miao Christians to reach the Nosu. Despite looking down on the A-Hmao and other Miao tribes for centuries, the Nosu had not failed to notice the dramatic change that had come into the Miao communities after they embraced Christ. Many Nosu wanted to experience the same peace and joy as their former slaves.

One factor holding back the growth of the Nosu churches in Guizhou at this time was the absence of Scripture in their language. Portions of the Bible had been translated into a special Nosu script in 1913, but these were for use among the Nosu in Sichuan and Yunnan. The Nosu in Guizhou spoke a different language and the script was never taught in the province.

An outdoor service of White Nosu Christians in 1937, led by a Black Nosu preacher

Pastor Wu and the precious Book

Decades passed, and as the political environment in China began to thaw in the late 1970s, the new freedoms triggered a growth in the Nosu Church. People no longer felt that becoming a Christian might cost them their lives, and the strong witness of the believers in their midst resulted in an ever-widening circle of Nosu Christians.

One of the centers of Nosu Christianity in Guizhou became Longyin Township in Pu'an County, where believers belonging to the Panxian Nosu group have met in three large house churches since 1980. One observer noted, "The Christians are held in high esteem by their neighbors because of their constant display of public spirit."[11]

In 1986, a 72-year-old Chinese pastor, Wu Liwen, was invited to a remote area in Guizhou by a group of Nosu people. The only question his hosts asked when they met Wu was if he knew who Jesus was.

Wu, who had spent 23 years in prison because of his faith in Christ, prayerfully sought God's will and felt it was right for him to make the arduous journey, even though it involved a hard uphill trek and a long donkey ride over treacherous mountain trails—challenges that people of his advanced age didn't usually undertake.

Wu's Nosu guides led him to a run-down shack in an isolated mountain range, which was to be their home for the night before his hosts took him to speak to their friends and relatives the next day. Wu expected a small gathering of perhaps 10 to 15 people.

After a rough night's sleep, the new day dawned and Wu was told they must climb over several more steep hills before they reached their destination. After straining for hours, the group finally cleared the last rise and suddenly heard voices:

Hundreds and hundreds of them! Sloping away beneath them, the mountainside rippled in a sea of blue and white—the tribal dress of the Nosu people. Like a late blooming of wildflowers, they covered every open space . . .

Some had traveled for days. Others had left their home villages long before daylight. Since no one wanted to miss a word, they came early. Pastor Wu learned that they had been assembled, waiting and watching the trail, for over six hours.

Wu scanned the crowd with tears in his eyes. His mind flashed back to the 23 years he spent in a Communist prison camp. During his darkest moments God had often spoken, telling him to hold on, for the time would come when he would be needed to teach the Word again. That promise had seemed so impossible! But here before him stretched 1,500 believers who had never had a teacher—waiting for him!

The hours rolled by into the night and still the old pastor taught. They lit torches and gas lanterns. No one wanted to leave. At last, Pastor Wu's voice gave out and they allowed him to stop and sleep.[12]

The exhausted pastor was finally taken to a nearby hut where he was given a hot meal and a bed for the night. Before falling asleep, however, Wu insisted on hearing the story behind the multitude of hungry believers he had just ministered to. His hosts laughed and said, "Let Old Lee tell you . . . He can tell you about the Book."

An aged blind man emerged from the back of the room and gently sat down on a low stool before Pastor Wu. Old Lee's battered face radiated an inner joy. In his arms he cradled a wooden box, holding it closely to his chest as if it contained a priceless treasure. "Teacher Wu," he began:

> "Thirteen years ago, no one in this village knew about God. My brothers and I spent most of our time drinking and gambling. We did not understand anything else. One day, I went down the

mountain with my brother to beg and to steal. In the market-place someone handed me this book."

Carefully, Old Lee extracted his prized possession. A small sheaf of coarse, brittle pages, long since yellowed and cracked, trembled in his hands. The pages were crudely stitched together, bound between two squares of dirty cardboard. Old Lee gently placed the book in the teacher's hands. Smiling and nodding, the villagers murmured their approval . . . "It is part of something called Matthew," Old Lee offered. "Of course, we didn't know what it was when we got it. But we decided it must be some kind of special book, so we hid it."[13]

The precious New Testament was concealed for years during the latter part of the Cultural Revolution, when a person could be killed for owning such a book. They placed it in a secret hiding place, and wondered if they would ever have an opportunity to learn more about its mysterious message.

The breakthrough they needed came when Old Lee was forced to attend a government propaganda meeting with people from several villages in the area. A Communist official made a long speech in which he ranted against religion. At one point he said, "The Christians claim that a man named Jesus Christ came to save mankind. This overseas religion was brought here to deceive us."

Old Lee remembered nothing else from the man's ramblings that day, but he was desperate to learn more about this person Jesus Christ. He instinctively knew that the old book in his possession was a Book of Truth, and he was determined to get help from someone able to read Chinese so they could understand its message. Old Lee continued:

At first, it was just the three of us. We hid the book in an empty shed, buried in the wall. Later, we brought a few others to read it, one at a time. Soon, 10 of us were believers and we met in the forest at night to encourage one another and pray. We became 30, then 50 and 60 . . .

As you can see, our numbers have grown . . . There are 1,500 of us now! Previously, we worshipped demons. Now only one family in our valley is not Christian, but they no longer worship demons either. We have heard about baptism. Do you know how to baptize?[14]

The news quickly spread throughout the village, and people ran to the hillside to break the news to those working in the fields: "We're going to be baptized!"

That afternoon a multitude of excited believers made their way to a stream where Pastor Wu baptized almost a thousand Nosu tribespeople. The next day he baptized hundreds more in a neighboring village. After two more days of teaching from morning till night, it was time for the venerable Bible teacher to return home.

Pastor Wu went to be with Jesus Christ a few years later, but the last phase of his life was spent testifying about the faithfulness of God, and how the Lord had kept His promise made during Wu's lowest point in prison many years earlier.

The Nosu today

Although the size of the Church among the Nosu in Guizhou has always paled in comparison to the massive revival among the neighboring Miao tribes, God has nonetheless done a powerful work among the Nosu. Because of government persecutions against Christianity in the 1960s and 1970s, many Nosu churches in Weining County went underground, where believers met secretly in small prayer and Bible study groups. In 1988, when national policies were relaxed, 15 Nosu churches reopened in Weining.

The congregations continued to grow, with one researcher noting in the late 1990s: "In northwest Guizhou the concentration of Christians among the minorities is sometimes very high. For instance, Geda village in Hezhang has 65 Nosu families, of which 57 are Christian."[15]

The Nosu believers have been called to endure many harsh trials and persecutions over the decades, but God preserved a faithful remnant for His glory, and today many strong churches exist among the Nosu of northwest Guizhou.

1950s and 1960s

Anointed for burial

The People's Republic of China was established on October 1, 1949, and the 1950s commenced with great uncertainty for the Church in Guizhou. Whereas in other parts of China some Christians expected the new government to usher in an era of freedom, few church leaders in Guizhou held such hopes. The province had already spent two decades being torn apart by the Communists, and their brutal suppression of the body of

A Chinese street preacher in the early 1950s

Christ promised a grim future now that they had control of the whole country.

Before the decade got underway, however, God opened a window of blessing for a short time. As the sun was setting on the era of foreign missionaries in China, Leslie Lyall was involved with large evangelistic youth rallies in Guizhou, which saw unprecedented openness to the gospel. He wrote:

> No one had ever seen the like. In two centers in Guizhou, an open-air campaign resulted in 220,000 people hearing the gospel in the course of 57 hours of preaching. In one meeting, 5,000 people stood in the rain for three hours listening intently.[1]

Looking back, it appears that this brief time of blessing may have been God anointing His Church in Guizhou for burial. The unexpected visitation from heaven helped fortify many for the trials that lay ahead. The impact of the meetings reverberated, and growth was experienced among the Chinese churches throughout the province. At Zunyi, the Christians had been deeply discouraged by their lack of progress. There was disunity among the believers, and many hidden sins in the congregation had grieved the Holy Spirit and prevented Him from blessing their work. The church reached its lowest point in 1950, causing some members to cry out to the living God for deliverance and mercy. Later that year, missionary Margery Sykes wrote from Zunyi:

> We did nothing but pray, and love them with His love, and the Lord did all the rest . . . Real unity now exists among the church leaders . . . The result is spiritual blessing of the first order. Once again folk are coming in and getting saved, and the 37 new believers baptized in September are going right on with the Lord.[2]

The Bosshardts' return

Many foreign missionaries had already left Guizhou by the start of the decade, and most of those who remained were arrested in 1950 or 1951 and expelled from China.

After the Swiss missionary Rudolf Bosshardt survived 560 days in Communist captivity from 1934 to 1936, many assumed that he and his wife Rose would quietly retire to their homeland. The Bosshardts were made of tough material, however, and after a time of recovery and sharing their testimony throughout Europe, they returned to Guizhou in 1940 and continued the work God had called them to.

The Bosshardts were highly respected, and many people were attracted to them and their message of the Savior. A small team of local Christians joined them, and the Holy Spirit pressed the needs of the unevangelized eastern districts of the province on their hearts. Rudolf had spent months walking through Hmu tribal areas during his captivity a decade earlier,

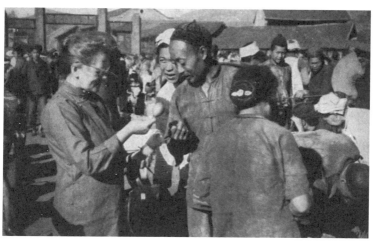

Rose Bosshardt in the marketplace at Panxian

and he retained a burning desire to return one day to reach them with the gospel.

A young Chinese missionary volunteered to make a journey throughout eastern Guizhou to survey the region. After weeks of traveling through the remote mountains, she gave this grim assessment: "In that area there are nearly 300 market towns and at least 600,000 people. So far as we know there is just one Protestant Christian there."[3]

As militant Communism swept across China and Mao Zedong commenced his totalitarian rule as the country's leader, thousands of missionaries either willingly left China or were forcibly removed. The Bosshardts, however, knew how to endure great hardship, Rudolf even having participated in the Red Army's Long March. They remained at their station in western Guizhou, courageously carrying on their work, even as the number of missionaries in China dwindled to just a tiny fraction of what it had previously been.

It is fitting that the last word on the foreign missionary era in Guizhou should come from the bold and persistent Bosshardts. In March 1951, with harsh persecution breaking out against believers everywhere, they filed their final report from Panxian, which told of a fresh receptivity among the people:

> The degree to which homes and hearts are open is ample justification for remaining on . . . The friendliness of the people, of all classes, is most marked. Attendances at the meetings have been well maintained, though recently we have noted a falling off of outsiders. On the other hand, old enquirers are beginning to return again after a lapse, sometimes of years. The men's side of the work has been strengthened by the conversion of several mature, well-educated men. As we baptize in the river, generally before a tremendous crowd, this step means much for these men. Financially, at least at present, these additional members mean little to the church, for all the new members have fallen

on lean days. It has been a great joy to see two or three making rapid progress spiritually. One man specially gives us great joy by the freshness of his testimony.[4]

A short time later, Rudolf and Rose Bosshardt were also forced to leave China, and the curtain was abruptly drawn on the era of foreign missions, nearly 200 years after the first Catholics had arrived in the province.

Typically, the Bosshardts refused to give up. They relocated to the Southeast Asian country of Laos, where they preached the gospel among the Chinese community for many years. Rose passed away in 1965, and Rudolf returned to England and settled in Manchester, where he founded the Manchester Chinese Christian Church. After a long and fruitful life dedicated to the service of Jesus Christ, Rudolf Bosshardt finally died in 1993, at the age of 96.

The worst persecution in Chinese history

Once the foreigners had been removed, persecution against the local Christians in Guizhou was unleashed with full force. Two pastors, Li Yuehan (John Lee) and Zhu Shiguang, were arrested and mercilessly tortured. Their treatment was so severe that Li died in prison within a few weeks, while Zhu's mind snapped due to the inhumane abuse he received from the Communist tormentors, and he committed suicide in 1951.

The campaign of terror continued, and in the mid-1950s the senior A-Hmao church leader, Zhu Huanzhang, was attacked during the government's "campaign to root out counter-revolutionaries" because he refused to renounce his faith in Christ. Zhu was diabolically tortured and pushed beyond the point of no return, and was driven to commit suicide in 1956.

At this time, with all foreigners removed from Guizhou, a black curtain descended, and for many years little or no news

*Christians from the Gha-Mu tribe were harshly persecuted in the 1950s
and beyond*
Paul Hattaway

emerged from the Christians in China's Precious Province. Nobody knew if the believers were being obliterated or were still meeting, and all that Christians around the world could do was pray and trust that the heavenly Father was sustaining his children, and that the wonderful revivals that had swept so many thousands of people into his kingdom would not go to waste.

The 1960s witnessed the worst persecution of Christians in Chinese history, especially during the decade-long Cultural Revolution which commenced in 1966. Church leaders were the hardest hit, with one survivor later describing the carnage:

> Thousands of pastors and devoted believers died because they stood firm in their faith. Additional thousands were sent to

prison where they suffered various forms of torture, hard labor and starvation. The government of China gave an edict which stated that if anyone was found spreading the gospel, they would be thrown into prison or put to death. Everywhere, believers were watched and much more.[5]

The cruel and creative methods used to torture and kill God's children during these dark years revealed the diabolic forces behind the evil acts. One pastor was arrested and severely tortured in an attempt to make him denounce Christ. When he steadfastly refused to do so:

> They became so angry with him that they brought a coffin and made him lie in it. They told him, "All right, now you must make a final decision! Either deny Jesus Christ or we will bury you." His only reply was, "I will never deny my Lord."
>
> They nailed the coffin shut and left it sitting for a time, listening for a voice from the inside. There was none. They

An A-Hmao family reading their treasured Bibles in Guizhou
RCMI

151

screamed and shouted at him and pounded on the casket. Still, only the sound of quiet, peaceful breathing. They buried him alive.[6]

The massive growth of the Miao churches in Guizhou was well known at the time, both in the Christian world and in Communist circles. Predictably, the tribal believers were targeted by the God-hating authorities, and numerous campaigns were launched in an attempt to "re-educate" the A-Hmao and Gha-Mu believers to stop them believing in "superstition."

The truth had been deposited deep within believers' hearts, however, and thousands of copies of the A-Hmao New Testament had been printed in 1937, 1947 and 1950. The precious Scriptures were spread over a wide area of Guizhou and Yunnan provinces just prior to the outbreak of persecution.

Believers in hundreds of villages now had cherished copies of God's Word, and they were determined not to lose them. During the worst of the anti-religious persecutions of the 1960s and 1970s, the A-Hmao hid their Bibles in obscure places, perhaps still motivated by the belief that they had once possessed a written language only to have lost it during a previous persecution.

Growth in the midst of adversity

Intense and sustained persecution was fully unleashed on the tribal churches in western Guizhou, and it was years before any news filtered through from the isolated mountains to the outside world. One Chinese researcher summarized the experiences of Guizhou's tribal churches with these words:

> The Miao teacher Yang Zhicheng and 162 other evangelists and Christians were labelled a "counter-revolutionary clique" and were wrongly sentenced to labor camps. In 1964, local cadres

investigated one production brigade which had more than 100 Christians and decided the church had taken over power from the grass-roots Party organs. Suppression of religion redoubled. All the ordained preachers suffered restrictions, which gave independent evangelists their opportunity.

In 1965 in Weining there were at least 647 independent (house church) preachers—more than 20 times the number of those formerly appointed in the original church.[7]

The continued growth of the tribal churches infuriated the Communist leaders, who were under pressure from Beijing to obliterate Christianity from the province. The launch of the Cultural Revolution in 1966 afforded an opportunity for the Communists to get rid of the Church once and for all, and nothing was held back. From the onset:

All religious believers were labelled "ghosts, snakes and monsters" and "running dogs of the imperialists". Some were forced to renounce their faith at special indoctrination sessions. In the Wumeng area alone, these sessions were held 18 times. Church buildings were confiscated and Bibles burnt.

When brute force didn't work, the government chose a new strategy to break the spirit of the tribal believers. In the village of Xiaoshiqiao ("Little Stone Bridge"), Christians were faced with a stark choice in 1969. They were told to choose between Jesus Christ and Chairman Mao, but warned that if they chose Christ they would face dire consequences. A local official announced, "The land belongs to Mao. You cannot till it. The cattle belong to Mao. You cannot pasture them. Every blade of grass belongs to Mao."[8]

Church leaders were dragged off to prison and endured unmentionable cruelties. Many were murdered or lost their minds due to the intensity of the torture they received. Those who remained in the villages were forced to give up their tiny plots of land, which provided their only source of food.

Concerned relatives and Christian brothers and sisters from other villages smuggled food to them under the cover of darkness.

Despite the widespread and brutal persecution, faith in Jesus Christ could not be uprooted from the hearts of the thousands of A-Hmao, Gha-Mu, Nosu and other tribal believers. Though buffeted by the storm, they stood firm and refused to abandon the living God. They drew strength from the promises of the Bible, and the second coming of Christ was often taught to give hope to the discouraged and downtrodden saints.

By the end of the 1960s, the body of Christ in Guizhou was battered and bruised. Hundreds of pastors had been sent to prison labor camps where many perished and were never heard from again, but the Communists had failed in their attempts to wipe out Christianity. In fact, there were indications that the faith had continued to spread, and the number of believers throughout the province may have even increased by the supernatural hand of God!

1970s

By the early 1970s, China had become a place of misery for the masses. Disastrous economic policies had led to the starvation of tens of millions of people. The leaders of the Communist regime, humiliated by their own failed ideology, launched wave after wave of horrific attacks against their own people in a bid to consolidate their power, and an atmosphere of fear and paranoia affected families throughout the country.

In the midst of this harsh environment, the Holy Spirit was still at work in Guizhou, drawing men and women with open hearts to Jesus Christ. A number of conversions of Red Guards occurred at the time, causing much consternation among Communist officials.

An A-Hmao church in Guizhou
RCMI

One young woman, who had joined the Red Guards while still at high school, was sent to be trained as a nurse. During an assignment at a local hospital, she was told to "change the thoughts" of an outstanding Christian doctor named Shi. She thought the task would be relatively straightforward, and that before long she would have persuaded him to abandon his faith.

The first step for the young woman was to discover all she could about the doctor's background, examining his strengths and probing his weaknesses. She discovered he had been raised in a loving Christian home by his widowed mother and three siblings. At university he had topped his class, and was liked and respected by both the faculty and his fellow students. Over time, the young Red Guard spent many hours with the doctor, and she later said:

> Our friendship progressed, and before long I realized I was falling in love with him. I knew my responsibilities as a member of the Party and it was my duty not to let my feelings get the better of me.
>
> I was having an inward struggle. I both wanted Dr. Shi to renounce his Christian faith and I wanted him as my husband . . . One thing perplexed me. Whenever he talked about the things he believed, he had assurance and power and I was unable to stand up to him . . . He refused to renounce his faith. I was all the more confused. If Christianity was false as I had been taught, why was Dr. Shi so strong? Marx said that religion was only for the weak.
>
> In spite of my opposition to his beliefs, he continued to be loving and caring toward me. Although his mother had been arrested for preaching the gospel, he bore no grudge but just praised God. Moreover, his mother in prison was not anxious or afraid of death. How could this be?[1]

The young Communist woman was confused, and the witness and prayers of Dr. Shi gradually broke through her resistance and the scales fell from her eyes. She realized that Communism was an empty philosophy with no real answers to life's problems, and she believed that Jesus Christ alone could bring salvation and deliver people from their sins. She humbled her heart and surrendered to God.

The young woman who had been trained to lead the Christian doctor away from his faith herself became a disciple of Christ. Years later, she summed up her life from that point on:

> I, a Communist Party member, became a Christian and a member of God's family. I thank God that He sent such a strong Christian to lead me into the truth. Dr. Shi and I were eventually married. As a result of my conversion I was expelled from the Communist Party. We were both sent "down to the country" to work in a health clinic, but we saw God's hand in this. Life was hard but we had many opportunities to serve the country people and to share the Lord Jesus with them.[2]

A barbaric massacre

The low point of the Communist brutality against Christians in Guizhou occurred in 1974, when a secret prayer meeting of A-Hmao and Gha-Mu believers at Xinlong Commune in Weining County culminated in the barbaric massacre of hundreds of defenseless believers. The massacre occurred during Mao's crazed "exterminate religion" campaign. The local Christians were sternly warned to abandon their meetings and renounce their faith, but they refused to comply, and they boldly told their oppressors:

> The more you forbid Christianity, the more we will cling to the Church. If you confiscate our buildings, we will worship in caves. If you announce the termination of our services, we will develop even more secret meetings. If you attack ordained pastors, we will use even more independent house church

Brother Zhang, an A-Hmao evangelist, preaching in a cave church

preachers instead. If you take action against us on Sundays, we
will meet every day of the week and into the night.[3]

This direct challenge to the authority of the Communist Party
was more than the officials could tolerate, and when they
learned of a large prayer gathering scheduled to take place in
a cave on Sunday, July 28, 1974, armed troops were mobilized.
They took up positions outside the entrance to the cave before
unleashing their machine guns and grenades on the unarmed
Christians, many of whom remained on their knees in a
posture of prayer as their lives were brought to an end.

When news of the slaughter spread throughout the region,
believers were shocked and they grieved deeply for their
dead brothers and sisters. Slowly, as the weeks passed, the
effect of the massacre was not one of fear and trembling
among the Christian community, but rather the example of the

slaughtered believers brought great strength and boldness to the body of Christ.

In hundreds of villages throughout the mountains of Guizhou and beyond, tribal believers made fresh commitments to the Lord Jesus Christ, and they redoubled their efforts to reach the lost. One observer noted, "The persecutions strengthened the Christian movement and led to a significant number of conversions. The number at least doubled according to local church leaders in Guizhou."[4]

A decade of destruction

After the massacre at Xinlong and the subsequent revival in many A-Hmao and Gha-Mu villages, the persecution didn't cease, and waves of diabolic hatred continued to roll in against Guizhou's minority believers during the remainder of the 1970s.

In March 1978, the authorities launched another campaign against those they described as "counter-revolutionaries hiding under the cloak of religion." Not for the first time, Xiaoshiqiao village was targeted for special treatment. News later emerged of how:

> Two hundred militia armed with rifles and machine-guns surrounded the village and demanded that they give up their faith in Christ. There was no answer, so the militiamen charged up the hill and took all the men in the village prisoner. They were trussed up like pigs and carried down to the town jail. The village head was sentenced to seven years in jail but was released after only one year. Eventually the cadres apologized to the people . . . The Christians replied, "We do not blame you at all. These events fulfil what is prophesied in the Bible. Christians must suffer. The gate to heaven is narrow."[5]

The following year, 1979, brought more sorrow and pain for the Miao Christians at Stone Gateway, when an evangelist,

Zhang Youxue, was arrested and tortured to death. His two sons, Zhang Mingcai and Zhang Mingan, were hunted like wild animals, and in an attempt to escape their pursuers they jumped into a river and drowned. This incident also caused many lukewarm believers to return to the churches, and once again the result was an increase in the number of Christians.

The 1970s was a terrible decade of destruction for the churches of Guizhou, yet by the supernatural hand of God, the body of Christ had survived the onslaught.

Left confused and red-faced by 30 years of failed attempts to obliterate the Church, the government had been taught the same lessons that Pharaoh experienced many centuries earlier. The Bible says of the Israelites in Egypt, "The more they were oppressed, the more they multiplied and spread" (Exodus 1.12). The same dynamic had occurred among the Church in Guizhou in the 1970s.

1980s

The unstoppable A-Hmao Church

After the death of Mao and the end of the Cultural Revolution in 1976, the 1980s dawned with Christians hoping for greater freedom to worship. The A-Hmao believers continued to be poor by the standards of this world, but their faith had been refined like pure gold. One visitor said of the A-Hmao believers in 1987:

> They witness to God, not by appearance, but by their living. Their mouths are not filled with theological terms or Biblical messages. Pastors do not wear ties, white shirts and dark blue pants; nor do they carry the Bible with them everywhere. What they wear are work clothes; what they carry are agricultural tools. They carry bamboo baskets with heavy loads on their backs . . .

The A-Hmao congregation at Banpo in 1987

> The A-Hmao Christians are a blessed community. They follow Christ family by family. Around 80 percent of the villagers are believers. This enables them to enjoy the blessings of God's life in a community of fellowship.[1]

Harsh persecution of the Christians among the A-Hmao and other Miao tribes commenced in the early 1950s and continued in waves for the next 30 years. Instead of decimating the churches as the authorities expected, however, the persecution had been the catalyst for massive growth in the number of A-Hmao believers, as one researcher found:

> In 1950 in the Hezhang District of Guizhou there were 9,800 Miao Christians meeting in 50 churches, according to a local government report. By 1986 they had grown to 23,000 believers meeting in 90 churches . . . The government also discovered that in 1986 the Miao believers in Wumeng had grown 10-fold from about 3,000 in 1950 to 30,000.[2]

An encouraging report noted that revival had impacted several different people groups: "Through it all, the church has moved forward. In the Wumao mountain area of Guizhou Province, Christians were estimated to be 70,000. This number includes A-Hmao, Gha-Mu, Hmong Shua, and some Nosu."[3]

Because of the large number of A-Hmao people who started following Jesus Christ throughout the 1970s and 1980s, it was deemed necessary to print 20,000 copies of their New Testament in 1983. These were soon put to good use, and an additional 30,000 copies were printed to meet the demands of additional new believers in 1988.[4]

House church missionaries arrive in Guizhou

For more than a century the Evangelical churches in Guizhou had largely been cut off from their counterparts in the rest

A Chinese believer kneeling in fervent prayer
RCMI

of China. There was little regular interaction between the Christians in Guizhou and other provinces, but the 1980s saw the emergence of large and powerful house church networks in eastern and central China. The Holy Spirit anointed those networks in such a mighty way that they quickly grew to contain millions of believers, and God gave them a vision to reach all of China. Naturally, it was a matter of time before they sent missionaries to Guizhou.

One of the largest and most fervent house church networks was the Born-Again Movement (also known as the Word of Life Church), which had been founded by Peter Xu Yongze. Years later, Xu told the author about the first workers his church sent to Guizhou:

> In 1986 our first workers arrived in Guizhou after graduating from our Bible school. When the teacher laid out a map of China before the class, some of the students prayed and

received a call from God to minister in Guizhou. They bought one-way train tickets and we laid hands on them in prayer, entrusting them to God's care.

When they arrived in the province it was raining heavily. The young men didn't know anyone and were at a loss as to what to do next. The Lord intervened by sending an elderly Christian woman to help them. She found them sheltering from the rain under a bridge and took them to live in her home while they figured out their next steps.

One of the workers who went to Guizhou was an elderly man named Guo Chang, who had read the Bible through more than 100 times. God used him greatly. On one occasion, Guo and a team of evangelists were trekking through the mountains in Liupanshui when they came across a gang of bandits. These evil men attempted to tie up Guo while they raped the female evangelists.

Old Brother Guo could not stand by and let them do this, so he started to fight them *kung fu* style. According to the women, the Spirit of God came upon Guo, and he was able to defeat four of the young men by himself. They ran away in absolute terror!

Even though he was able to thwart their wicked plans, one of the bandits slashed Brother Guo's face with a knife, resulting in permanent hearing loss. The women prayed for him, but they had no medicine to treat the injury. Guo lived another few years before passing away.[5]

The widely respected China church expert Jonathan Chao provided more details of this dangerous incident. He wrote:

A group of itinerant evangelists consisting of five men and two women were attacked by a bandit group. Suddenly bandits appeared and attacked the girls. The two men in front distracted the bandits, wanting the girls to escape. In their fury the bandits drew big knives and attacked the two evangelists, intending to kill them. One of the brothers, who had served in the army and learned some *kung fu* as a youth, was able to avoid the flashing saber and was even able to overcome the attacker, grabbing his long knife. However, in the midst of this life-and-death struggle, a second man knifed him from behind with a fruit knife.

When the robbers were defeated they quickly ran away, leaving their knives on the ground. The evangelists then continued their journey, though one of them was badly wounded.[6]

The Three-Self churches start afresh

The government-sanctioned Three-Self Church in China gained a terrible reputation among sections of the Chinese

The impressive Three-Self church at Bijie in northwest Guizhou

Church between its founding in 1951 and the end of the 1970s, when many Three-Self pulpits were filled by Communist officials who gave political and patriotic speeches instead of teaching from the Bible.

In many places, the atheistic government-appointed pastors in the registered churches were widely known to have betrayed Jesus Christ and His followers. Some had even been personally involved in the persecution of house church leaders, having them arrested, tortured and thrown into prison for years.

The independent house church believers saw it as ludicrous and disgraceful that such people could ever be considered leaders of God's flock, and they strongly opposed the Three-Self Patriotic Movement (TSPM)—a stance that continues for millions of house church Christians to the present day.

By the early to mid-1980s, however, a relaxation of the government's religious policies promised to thaw the frosty relationship between the state and the body of Christ. Throughout Guizhou, the members of underground churches were faced with a difficult decision—whether to remain hidden or to risk trusting a government that had ruthlessly persecuted them for decades.

The leaders of many house churches decided that registering their congregations was a step too far, and they remained independent and outside government control. Others, however, thought it was time for change, and they believed the potential benefits of registering would outweigh the risks.

Many Christians in Guizhou's Gebu County decided to register. Their churches had grown steadily over the years, and they believed it was the right pathway to pursue. In 1986, "14 Miao pastors, 26 elders and 27 preachers were ordained at Gebu, which indicates a healthy, growing church. By May 1990, a group of 500 Christians crammed into one church where 80 were awaiting baptism."[7]

How the churches grew

By the late 1980s the Church in Guizhou was experiencing strong growth among both the Han Chinese majority and the myriad of colorful minority groups scattered throughout the province. During a discussion with an elderly Chinese house church pastor named Wu and his wife, a visitor had his conversation interrupted by three young men who had just arrived from a distant mountain village. They were covered in dirt and glistening with sweat, and looked like they hadn't slept for days. They immediately asked Wu, "Do you have any Bibles?"

Desperate believers had sent the three young men hundreds of miles by truck and train to find Bibles. The pastor filled their bags with copies of God's Word and told them where they could obtain more. The visitors were overjoyed!

After the men gave thanks to God and commenced their long journey home, Pastor Wu resumed the conversation by sharing how the Holy Spirit had given strategies to believers which enabled them to reach people more effectively for Jesus Christ. Although it wasn't possible to preach on the streets in China or pass out literature without being arrested, he explained:

> The people invite us into their homes, especially in rural areas, where 20 to 30 will often gather to hear the gospel in an open courtyard. Most of them want to be prayed for because they have a relative or friend who has been healed through prayer. In these circumstances we have to write down their names and pray for the people in the order they are listed. God is so good. He honors their faith and usually about 70 percent of the sick are healed.
>
> When a miracle of healing takes place, a whole family will believe. Sometimes that includes many relatives living in the same village. Then we will have a special service in their main courtyard when we burn the idols the family has been

167

worshipping. Superstition and idol worship are just as common as before the Communist revolution in rural areas, and so is fear and dread of evil spirits. But deliverance comes with the preaching of Christ and His resurrection. So the message has spread far and wide.

When these new believers have a wedding or a first-month birthday celebration for a new baby, they invite us to speak to the guests. They especially want us to attend funerals. On all of these occasions, the Christians take part, sharing their faith with the large numbers of people in attendance. The authorities make no objection when the gospel is spread this way.[8]

Pastor Wu personally encountered many trials and persecutions for the gospel during his years of ministry, but the Holy Spirit always gave him words to say at crucial times. Once, Wu was arrested in a remote area of Guizhou for distributing Bibles. When he returned home to the capital city, the police interrogated him. When they demanded to know if he had handed out Bibles to people, he boldly replied, "Yes, I gave Bibles to the Christians. Some were very poor and we gave them money and clothing, too. Is there anything wrong with that?" The police officers felt ashamed and didn't say another word.

Going the extra mile

The Christians in Guizhou often gained favor with people and with government officials because of the practical help they rendered. In one area, when a section of public road needed repair, the Communist cadre in charge of the project divided the work crew into two groups—Christians and non-Christians. Both started work at the same time, but the believers worked well together and finished their section of the road long before the others, so they joined forces with the non-believers and stayed until the work was completed.

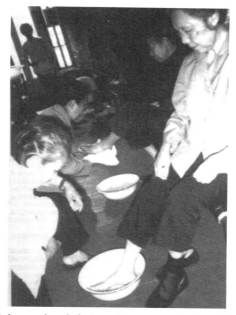

A house church foot-washing service in the 1980s

In another part of the province, a new Christian boarded a bus and asked to buy 30 tickets. "Why so many?" asked the surprised vendor. She replied, "I have been riding this bus many times without paying my fare. Now I am a Christian and I want to pay what I owe."[9]

"What is a Christian?" the ticket seller asked. "What kind of person would do such a thing?" An invitation was given to learn more about Jesus Christ, which the ticket seller gladly accepted.

Letters from Guizhou

By the late 1980s many letters were being received by Christian ministries in Hong Kong and elsewhere, shedding light on the situation and needs of the body of Christ in China. While hundreds of letters poured in from across the country, very few were received from Guizhou. One reason was that most believers in the province were tribal Christians who were only able to read and write their own language.

One letter which did emerge from Guizhou in 1986 revealed a desperate need:

> I am a young believer. We have many Christians in the Miao tribe and we now have our own church. Though I am a Christian, I don't have a Bible. I hear people talking about the Bible, but I personally have never even seen one. Could you please send me two Bibles, one being for another brother?[10]

Another letter emerged in 1989, revealing an urgent need for discipleship among Guizhou's Christians:

> Although I have been a Christian for 10 years, I have never left the elementary teachings about Christ. We lack shepherds and do not know how to press on to maturity. I decided to dedicate my whole family to Christ half a year ago, wishing we could live a victorious life every day. Nevertheless, I am still spiritually weak. Please pray for us.[11]

As the 1980s drew to a close, it was apparent that God was doing a deep and effective work in many parts of Guizhou. Although widespread revival had not yet broken out as it had in other provinces of China, the kingdom of God was quietly growing one believer at a time, and many whose lives had been transformed by the Holy Spirit were actively sharing the good news with their relatives and neighbors.

The suspicion that the gospel had been steadily gaining ground in Guizhou was confirmed in 1987, when an official publication estimated there were 100,000 believers just in the government-approved Three-Self churches in the province.[12] In addition, thousands of independent house churches had sprung up across Guizhou, which were believed to contain at least 250,000 believers at the time.

The Bouyei

A varied background

The Bouyei are the second largest ethnic minority group in Guizhou, numbering nearly three million people. They are found in large numbers throughout southern Guizhou, and they spill across the borders into Guangxi, Yunnan and other provinces. The center of the Bouyei region could be said to be China's largest waterfall, Hongguoshu, which is surrounded by numerous Bouyei villages.

A Bouyei woman in traditional dress
Paul Hattaway

Historically, the Bouyei are considered part of the great Tai race, which is dispersed from central China all the way to Southeast Asia, and as far west as northeast India. Although the centuries have caused the Tai race to fragment into separate entities with their own customs and languages, there remain unmistakable ethno-linguistic similarities between the various Tai peoples. The Bouyei of Guizhou, for example, share much in common with the Zhuang of Guangxi—the largest ethnic minority group in China with a population of nearly 20 million people.

The Bouyei themselves, however, often claim Han ancestry, and are not keen to identify themselves as a minority people. Missionary Samuel Clarke, who lived among them for decades, offered this theory regarding the historical background of the Bouyei:

> Wherever the Bouyei are found in Guizhou, they invariably assert that their ancestors were Chinese who came from the province of Jiangxi, and many of them name the prefecture and county from which their forefathers came . . .
>
> Before the Chinese really occupied the province and systematically colonized it, there had been frequent wars and military demonstrations against the turbulent Miao. There were also on these occasions garrisons left in different parts of the country. Some of these soldiers took native women as wives, and formed separate communities, and are now called the "Old Chinese." Others of them, or the children of these garrison soldiers, married into Bouyei families. This marrying probably went on for a long period, so that in course of time many of them were really descended from the Chinese, and others were related to them by marriage . . . As the Chinese are the superior and ruling race, it is natural that as many as can claim to be related to them should do so.[1]

The great Tai peoples of Southeast Asia adopted Buddhism many centuries ago, and their identities are now interwoven with the religion, making them difficult to reach with the gospel of Jesus Christ. In contrast, groups like the Bouyei remain largely animistic, with the Chinese influences of ancestor worship and Daoism mixed into their worldview.

Although animist peoples in Asia have generally been receptive to the claims of Christ and relatively easy to reach, the Bouyei have proven surprisingly difficult to penetrate with the gospel. Today, more than a century after missionaries first encountered them, less than 1 percent of Bouyei people are followers of Jesus.

Early contact

One of the reasons that Evangelical missionaries struggled to make inroads into the Bouyei people was because the Catholics had already focused on the Bouyei for a century before the first Protestants arrived. A fear of Christianity had emerged among the Bouyei after waves of brutal persecution and martyrdoms over the decades. The lingering impression among many Bouyei was that Christianity is a religion that brings calamity upon its adherents, and consequently few were willing to embrace it.

Curtis Waters of the CIM is believed to be the first Evangelical missionary to target the Bouyei. In 1891 he established a base in Xingyi. The mission didn't last long, however, with banditry and riots causing local officials to expel the missionaries from the area in 1902. Waters shifted his focus away from the Bouyei, and was involved with the A-Hmao revival that commenced a short time later.

Samuel Clarke, another CIM missionary, also made contact with the Bouyei in the late nineteenth century. He remarked:

> These people are difficult to reach. They live in separate communities generally away from the high roads. There are no inns

and no tea shops in their villages, and strangers are not welcome among them. The first time I visited one of their villages I was doubtful as to the reception I should meet, so to reassure them I took my wife with me. When we entered the place everybody disappeared, and all doors were closed. We called out for hot water and sat down on a doorstep. At last, seeing we were not likely to move till we got some hot water, some was given to us. We were treated much the same way when we visited them a second time, but as we continued to go, their fear of us gradually wore away.[2]

Samuel Clarke persevered, and spent more than 30 years serving Christ in Guizhou, although for much of the time he appears to have struggled with his feelings toward the Bouyei people. On one occasion Clarke unflatteringly wrote:

We do not think the claim of the Bouyei to be Chinese has done them any good. They appear to have all the defects of the Chinese and none of their better qualities . . . The Chinese generally describe the Bouyei as crafty, lying, and dishonest, and [say] that every Bouyei is a thief, and from what we know of them we should not feel justified in denying the charge.[3]

The Clarkes found that the Bouyei living near Guiyang were much easier to visit and more hospitable to foreigners than those in the remote settlements. They were able to rent a house in one Bouyei village, from where they visited other communities in the area. Discovering one of the greatest needs of the Bouyei was to educate their children, Clarke opened small schools in three villages, although he later lamented:

In the evening many of them come and listen to the gospel. Men from other places have also come and asked me to open schools in their villages. If we had men and means, there is apparently no limit to the number of places we could occupy this way . . .

Dictionaries of their language have also been made, and a catechism and tracts have been translated into it. These people, like the Miao, have no written language of their own. They are vastly amused and interested when we take out a book and begin to read to them in their own tongue. Most of the Bouyei I have met can speak Chinese, so it is not necessary that the missionary among them should learn their language.[4]

Before Samuel Clarke and his wife left the mission field for a furlough in 1898, they offered this grim prognosis of the Bouyei mission:

The work among them has not been very encouraging thus far. They all seem utterly indifferent to things spiritual . . . A few of them pretended an interest in the gospel and applied for baptism, but it was found in course of time that their thoughts were of the earth, and baptism was refused. Only three of them have been baptized, and these are by no means satisfactory.[5]

Although the Gospel of Matthew was first translated into the Bouyei language in 1904, outreach among minority groups in the province soon focused on several receptive Miao tribes where revival had broken out. The Bouyei were neglected, and it wasn't until 1919 that the next breakthrough was reported among them. Tellingly, Morris Slichter of the CIM (who was later murdered in 1927) seemed unaware of any previous Bouyei Christians when he wrote, "Six men were baptized. These are the first-fruits of the Bouyei tribe."[6]

Brief contact in the 1940s

As the revival continued among the A-Hmao and other groups, the success of that work seems to have sucked the oxygen out of other missionary efforts in the province, so that even large groups like the Bouyei remained almost completely untouched by the gospel. One missionary had lamented in 1934, "There are two million Bouyei in this province, and only about two Christians among them."[7]

In 1948, Cyril Edwards and his co-workers visited a Bouyei village near Ziyun. They arrived after dark, having hiked through mud and driving rain for hours. They entered a house and were drying out their soaked clothing and shoes as the Bouyei returned home from working in the fields. Edwards recalled:

> They did come, gradually, a couple of rooms full. At first they were very much amused at the idea of being preached to, but their interest was soon aroused in the gospel message . . . These Bouyei form a large part of the country population right across the south of this province, and nothing is being done to bring them the simple gospel message of salvation . . .
>
> From this district we walked east for five days without passing through one place where there are any Christians or where there is any Christian testimony. In fact, apart from one or two more educated Chinese who in other places had heard of Christianity, no one had ever heard the Name of Jesus![8]

The Bouyei today

With a population approaching that of entire countries like New Zealand and Norway, the Bouyei people remain severely unevangelized after more than a century of half-hearted efforts to introduce the gospel to them. Since the 1990s, a number of house church networks from other parts of China have attempted to reach the Bouyei, with moderate success.

Foreign Christians have also attempted to engage the Bouyei in the past few decades, but have generally found them to be uninterested in the gospel. Several teams traveled to Bouyei villages and began to show the *Jesus* film and distribute Christian

Many Bouyei women are skilled embroiderers
Paul Hattaway

literature, only to be arrested by the police. An American shared what happened after his small team was interrogated and ordered to leave the area:

> After packing our belongings, we stretched our hands out toward the unreached Bouyei homes. The valley was shrouded in a misty haze, pierced here and there by the early rays of sunlight. We prayed that God would watch over the lives of those who had expressed interest in the gospel; that He would cause the seeds that were sown to grow into a mighty harvest of souls. We prayed that there would be a spiritual awakening among this tribe, and that many of their names might be written in the Book of Life.[9]

Foreign and local Christians did not give up trying to reach the Bouyei, and in 2008 one mission group reported a breakthrough:

Everywhere we went, the favor of God was on us. The villagers were very open to us and the message of the gospel. Several Bouyei believers will be coming out of their area for training soon. I believe in a short time we will start to see Bouyei churches sprout up.[10]

Two years later the same group reported progress among the Bouyei, coupled with outreach to the Ge tribe in another part of Guizhou:

Among these two groups, we have already had a church-planting base for a year and a half. It was great being with the local brother who is running the operation on the ground. He has been very hard at work evangelizing and discipling new converts. It's amazing to see how God is using these local brothers and sisters to plant churches where there has never been any before.[11]

Although reports have indicated the presence of pockets of Bouyei believers in various locations, no widespread turning to Christ has ever occurred among this large group. Today there are an estimated 4,000 Evangelical Christians among the 2.6 million Bouyei, which means just one out of every 650 Bouyei people is a follower of Jesus Christ.

The almighty God has been patiently looking down from heaven for centuries, waiting for more of His ambassadors to visit the Bouyei and share the wonderful news that His beloved Son bled, died for their sins, and rose again for the justification of those who believe in Him.

1990s

Communists turn to Christ

Christianity in many areas of Guizhou continued to flourish throughout the 1990s. The decade saw a further softening in attitudes against the Church compared to the brute force used in previous decades, but life continued to be desperately hard for many tribal believers.

By 1995 the Communist Party had taken notice of the over-flowing churches, and they launched a campaign to prevent party members becoming Christians. The Hong Kong newspaper *Ming Bao* published a report which stated:

> Recently a large number of Communist Party members joined the ranks of Christianity in the Bijie District of Guizhou Province. According to a survey . . . in 1991 there were only 150 Party members who had joined the Church. But by 1995 the number exceeded 2,000. In Nayong County alone there were 23 Party members registered as church members, of whom 18 were cadres in national organizations. More than 100 Party members regularly attend church activities there . . .
>
> The survey revealed that Party members who became Christians were not just ordinary young people but old cadres who had been in the Party for decades . . . The Party Vice-Secretary in Zhijin County who had served in the 1950s and in the 1970s as Commune leader is now a leading light in the church.
>
> The conversion of leading Party members has led to the growth of Christianity by the thousands and the tens of thousands. The prestige of Party and local government organs has dropped. In some remote villages people obey the pastor rather than the village Party head.[1]

Stone Gateway revisited

In 1996, a small group of foreigners traveled to Shimenkan (Stone Gateway), hoping to visit the grave of the great missionary pioneer Samuel Pollard. Shimenkan had served as the center for the A-Hmao revival nearly a century earlier under Pollard's guidance. The group reported:

> It is still one of the poorest areas in China without a single paved road. The peasants still live in the same mud and straw huts, tending tiny patches of land among the steep mountains . . . The Nosu landlords have gone, many beaten to death during land reform in the early 1950s, but the A-Hmao seem as poor as when Pollard first met them. Locals say that up to 80 percent of the population do not earn enough to feed and clothe themselves . . .[2]

The visitors were concerned by some of the things they learned on their brief visit to Shimenkan. They discovered that very few

A rural church in northwest Guizhou
RCMI

A-Hmao children attended school, as their parents were unable to afford the annual school fees of about $240. One local told the group:

> "It was better before the Revolution. Many believe that there is no point sending their children to school if they just have to go back to the farm afterwards." Like other impoverished parts of China, locals believe central government subsidies are pocketed by corrupt local officials. "We don't have roads here but all the local officials have bought themselves expensive foreign jeeps."[3]

Because of the excruciating poverty in Guizhou, many A-Hmao young adults left the area in search of work in more developed parts of China. Whereas nearly every village family follows Jesus Christ and regularly attends church meetings, those who left the area found life much more complicated, with only about 30 percent of A-Hmao people living elsewhere managing to retain their faith.

A century earlier, Samuel Pollard had helped free the A-Hmao from slavery to the brutal Nosu landlords, but the visitors soon found that the Communist Party of the 1990s had assumed the role of oppressors of the A-Hmao people. Two of the Chinese men who accompanied the visitors were arrested and detained by the local authorities for bringing foreigners to see Pollard's grave. "We have our own power here and can do what we like," the corrupt officials boasted.

Startling growth throughout Guizhou

For a century, the jewels in the crown of the Guizhou Church had been the tribal Christians in the west of the province, whereas generations of Han Chinese and other tribal people had lived and died without believing in Jesus Christ.

The 1990s saw God's Spirit move among the Han Chinese and various neglected minority groups, however, and startling

A crowded tribal church in Guizhou

growth occurred in many parts of the province. Tony Lambert, highly regarded as an expert on Christianity in China, summarized the situation in Guizhou at the time:

In 1993 when I spoke to a leading TSPM pastor in Guiyang, the capital, he estimated there to be 300,000 to 400,000 believers— a 30 to 40-fold increase! The Miao area of Hezhang has seen growth from 4,000 believers to more than 26,000, meeting in 60 churches and meeting points . . .

In Liupanshui, 60 percent of the Christians are Miao [A-Hmao and Gha-Mu], 20 percent Nosu or Bouyei, and 20 percent Han Chinese. In Weining 9,000 are Miao, 7,000 are Nosu and the remainder mainly Han.

In northwest Guizhou the concentration of Christians among the minorities is sometimes very high . . . Some villages in Puding and Zhijin counties inhabited by A-Hmao are 95 percent Christian. In the Wumeng Mountains there are over 10,000 tribal believers meeting in several dozen churches . . .

Guizhou has large numbers of Christians, but the Church has a chronic shortage of educated leaders. In Hezhang, for example, 80 percent of the preachers have had only a primary school education.[4]

This overwhelming need for competent church leaders became a constant theme in communications from believers in Guizhou. One letter in 1998 said:

> For more than a year we have had no teaching. There is no church and the local authorities didn't allow us to set up study meetings, but now we have a small meeting-point of 40 people.[5]

Although at long last the light of the gospel was shining on the Han Chinese in Guizhou, many challenges remained. Although there were now more Christians to spread the gospel, the onslaught of materialism which engulfed China in the 1990s meant that the harvest had somewhat soured, with many people no longer interested in spiritual things as they set their minds to accumulating worldly possessions. One letter from Guizhou in 1999 encapsulated the difficulties facing the churches at the time:

> As we live in a mountainous region where transportation is very inconvenient, we have set up three meeting places with a total of 62 believers. The development of this area is very difficult because it is backward and we are a minority group that is deeply influenced by idols. Most families grow corn for a living. The people here live for money, and very few of them are interested in listening to our message.[6]

The spectacular growth of the Church in certain areas of Guizhou did not go unnoticed, with even government books remarking on the sudden expansion of Christianity in the province. In 1997, one official publication estimated that 50 percent of all Nosu people in Weining County had become Christians.[7]

Although estimates of the overall number of Christians in China fluctuated throughout the 1990s according to various sources, researcher Tony Lambert—a man known to favor a more conservative approach—consistently provided a figure of 300,000 to 400,000 Evangelical believers in Guizhou. These estimates revealed explosive growth since 1987, when 100,000 Evangelicals were reported in the province.[8]

By the end of the twentieth century it was apparent that God was doing a strong work throughout Guizhou, and the flame of the gospel promised to burn even more brightly as the new millennium commenced.

2000s

A decade of harvest

At the start of the new millennium, various short-term mission teams visited Guizhou from the United States, Singapore, Malaysia and other parts of the world. They conducted prayer walks through unreached areas, and discreetly shared the gospel when opportunities arose.

The Miao communities in eastern parts of the province were a favorite destination for mission teams. Not only were the Hmu and many other Miao tribes unreached and in urgent need of the gospel, but the people were extremely hospitable,

A Miao believer reading a Pollard script Bible
Miao Messenger

and their vibrant and colorful cultures created unforgettable memories for the visitors.

One team of Southern Baptists from America encountered many Miao people who were hungry to hear about Jesus. One young Miao woman was shocked to see a team of foreigners giving away their own food, water and items of clothing to poor villagers they met along the road. She chased after them and asked, "Why do you love them? You don't even know them. You don't even know me! I've never seen a love like this before."[1]

Another prayer team visited a market town in Guizhou when they were approached by a young Miao man who wanted to practice his English. The visitors were happy to oblige, and as they spoke he grew increasingly interested in their message about God. They shared deep into the night, and the young man gave his life to Christ. He said, "I know this is strange, but I see a bright light before me, and I see a Man telling me He loves me."[2]

The team left the town the next day, but some months later one of the intercessors returned to discover the man had led four of his friends to Jesus Christ! They had only one Chinese Bible, but were meeting together to read it. A church had been planted because of the visit of the American prayer team.

In another part of Guizhou lived a Miao man named Adam, who was blind in one eye. He was given a Chinese Bible by a foreign Christian, and when he read that Jesus healed blind people, he asked, "Do you really think this happened?" He wanted to believe in a God who had the power to heal and forgive, so he decided to give his life to Jesus Christ regardless of whether he received physical healing or not.

Adam returned to his home village, and a short time later he again visited his Christian friend. The foreigner took the opportunity to teach Adam about baptism. "Oh, I've already done that," Adam replied. "I read about it in the Bible, so I went out to the rice field and I got down in the water and said something like, 'Out with the old man, in with the new!' I dunked myself in the water and got back up. Was that okay?"[3]

The love of Christ breaks down barriers

After centuries of conflict and racial hatred between the Han Chinese and Miao in Guizhou, the burgeoning churches among both groups found unity around the cross of Jesus Christ, where grace and forgiveness abound.

A Miao evangelist, Brother Long, was invited to address a Chinese congregation in a large city, where he shared about his recent visit to poor Miao churches. After noting that in the past there had been no chance for him to speak to a gathering of Han Christians, Long declared:

> "Our faith in Christ has changed all that. In Christ, we are all one family." In this setting, marked by the Spirit's presence, the Miao brother felt at ease, a member of the family!
>
> Brother Long went on to describe his recent experiences in seven remote villages. He highlighted the desperate need of one village for a church building, and he detailed how believers in another place had started a much-needed school, but were struggling to keep the project afloat . . .
>
> When the service ended, the church gave over 5,100 Yuan (about US$610) toward the needs of the Miao Christians. In view of the fact that most of the Chinese believers earned about US$100 per month, this was a tremendous response.[4]

Blanket saturation

In the 2000s the Christian world seemed to awaken to the fact that large swathes of Guizhou remained completely unevangelized. God raised up both Chinese and foreign Christians with hearts to rectify the situation, and through a myriad of strategies the gospel went forth to multitudes of people who had never heard it before. One mission group felt called by God to blanket entire areas with gospel literature and evangelistic video and audio resources. In 2005 its members reported:

> We have witnessed to over 10,000 people this year in central Guizhou. Some of these homes take up to three days to reach by walking along mountain paths. The good news is that there are no police in these remote areas so we are very safe here. Sometimes we encounter a language barrier, but we carry minority language CDs with us. We plan to finish placing the gospel into all remaining 40,000 homes in the area by the end of the year.[5]

Many rural areas of Guizhou experienced strong church growth during this decade of harvest. Signs and wonders accompanied the preaching of the gospel, causing entire villages to believe in Jesus Christ. In one place, a woman had been demonized for years, causing great anguish to her family and disharmony to the entire community. Various cures had been tried, and local spirit-priests had been summoned to try to deliver the troubled woman, to no avail.

One day a small team of Christians visited from a nearby village, and when they heard the woman's tormented screams, they offered to pray for her. Most of the villagers gathered around to watch, and as the believers calmly prayed for her, the woman's fierce countenance changed and she became calm. After some time she was restored to normal and the people who witnessed it were amazed.

That day, 120 people in the village believed in Jesus Christ. In the year following the miracle some fell away, but 70 villagers continued to stand firm in the faith.

The martyrdom of Jiang Zongxiu

In June 2004, a 34-year-old Christian woman, Jiang Zongxiu, traveled to Tongzi County in northern Guizhou, where she

Jiang Zongxiu
China Aid

visited the market with her mother-in-law, Tan Dewei. Both women had been active house church workers for more than a decade.

Jiang and Tan, like the Biblewomen of an earlier era, distributed Bibles and gospel tracts to some of the stall owners and their customers. Most were appreciative, but some reported their activities to the authorities. The Public Security Bureau dispatched officers to the market and arrested the Christian pair. Jiang and Tan were handcuffed together and taken to the local detention center, where they were interrogated throughout the night of June 17 and into the following morning.

Jiang and her mother-in-law were sentenced to 15 days' imprisonment. The official police report listed the charge as "seriously disturbing the social order by distributing Christian literature to the masses in the market."[6] Before they had even commenced their sentence, however, police officers beat and kicked Jiang Zongxiu to death at around 2 p.m. on June 18, 2004. Ludicrously, the official reason for her death was given as a "sudden disease."

The authorities, afraid of the ramifications of murdering someone on such a minor charge, ordered Jiang's family to cremate the body immediately, and even sent an invoice demanding 100 Yuan (about $12) per day for the preservation of the corpse at the funeral home. Jiang's husband, Zhang Zhonghua, refused to pay and arranged for a full autopsy to be carried out to determine the cause of death.

The relatives of the martyred woman were deeply angered by the incident and publicized it widely. Even China's *Legal Daily*, a newspaper edited by the Chinese Department of Justice, reported the story and mocked the Tongzi officials' claims that Jiang had died of natural causes.

Numerous people signed affidavits stating that Jiang Zongxiu had been a strong and healthy young woman with no medical

Jiang Zongxiu's husband and four-year-old son grieving at her tomb
China Aid

problems. Even a police officer present at the autopsy said, "She doesn't need an autopsy, because it's very obvious that she was beaten to death."[7] Jiang's sister-in-law secretly took photos of the battered and bruised corpse. Much of her hair had been torn from her scalp. Relatives who saw Jiang's body in the funeral home all claim that they saw much blood on her body, and scars from beatings on her legs and neck. The publication of the photographs, as well as a video of family members outlining what had happened, caused great embarrassment and anger among the government officials, who threatened the family with retribution if they continued their campaign for justice.

Jiang Zongxiu had touched many lives for Jesus Christ. She left behind a loving husband, and a four-year-old son, Zhang Jun, who couldn't understand what had happened and frequently called out for his mother. Jiang's sister-in-law asked, "We are just ordinary Christians. All of our family is illiterate. We just want justice. They killed my sister because she was caught sharing her faith. Why did she have to die? Why does her four-year-old son have to grow up without a mother?"[8]

Humbled at a Miao worship service

As foreign Christians gained more access to China in the new millennium, some boldly traveled to remote tribal areas and enjoyed rich fellowship with believers who had been starved of contact with overseas Christians for decades. One Western believer, Luke Wesley, shared his experiences following a visit to a remote Miao village:

> I arranged for a van to take us as far up the mountain as possible. The village we were to visit was located in a remote and very poor area of the province. The road conditions were rough and finally, with a gasp, the driver pulled over and said that he had driven as far as possible. We would need to hike the rest of the way.

After a short hike, we arrived to the sort of welcome that only the Miao can give. Believers lined the path singing songs of welcome and encouragement. They led us in this manner into the church. Although the population of that village was less than 200, a sea of over 250 smiling faces had packed into the church . . .

The service began, and I was quickly reminded that there are few things as humbling as participating in a Miao worship service. You see, the Miao assume that everyone can sing. They are wonderful singers and their choirs are renowned for the exquisite beauty of their songs. It does no good to protest—visitors must always contribute at least one song . . .

Afterwards, the Miao choir assembled at the front and began to sing. The power and beauty of their worship was breathtaking. Our team sat in awe as these simple people from the mountains—a people who, prior to receiving the gospel a little over 100 years ago, were viewed as savages—sang songs that would have been welcomed in any cathedral in the world. And then their children's choir sang. It was wonderful . . .

After the singing came to an end, our team shared about God's love and His power to change lives . . . The message struck a chord in the hearts of the Miao and the entire congregation rose to their feet . . . The Spirit filled the place and many began to cry, shake and worship with a loud voice. It was Pentecost all over again, but this time in the mountains of China.

I had never seen anything like this in a Miao church. The Miao tend to be rather formal and reserved in manner and worship. But here, an incredible sense of hunger and openness to the things of the Spirit permeated the place. Formalities were laid aside as people entered into the presence of God.

In the midst of all this I noticed the driver of our van standing in the congregation and, with wide eyes, [he] was taking it all in. I walked over and asked him what he thought about all that was going on. He replied, "This is wonderful. I am deeply moved." I asked him if he knew Jesus. He replied, "No, not yet, but I am ready!"

The impact on him of God's presence and the authentic worship was evident. I shared the gospel with this man and then led him in the sinner's prayer. His face radiated with joy as we returned home that day.[9]

Breakthroughs among the unreached

While the churches among some minority groups in Guizhou had grown appreciably by the start of the twenty-first century, other tribes experienced the first-known Christian breakthroughs in their history. One of them was the little-known Mo tribe of about 20,000 people who inhabit an area on the southern Guizhou border with Guangxi.

In 1995, a Hong Kong-based mission organization visited the Mo and won several individuals to Christ. The new converts immediately started a house church, and about 30 more Mo people became Christians in the following few years.

The Ge tribe had first heard the gospel from Australian Maurice Hutton in the 1930s, but no Christian community endured among them. In 2002, a foreign believer was led by God to visit the Ge people. She traveled to their area numerous times, building relationships with key individuals and sharing the gospel when opportunities arose. After one of her visits to the Ge, she reported:

Before we knew it the Lord opened an opportunity to share. An old man and his wife and their elderly neighbor and daughter came and sat down with us. We shared about Jesus Christ as a young man translated for us from Mandarin into the Ge language. This was one of the most incredible moments of my whole year . . .

After we shared from creation to the Cross, the old man said he wanted to follow Jesus and the young man also professed faith in Him. I can only imagine what a sweet sound it was in the Father's ears to hear His name called upon in the Ge tongue.[10]

Three Ge girls in traditional dress
Paul Hattaway

The gospel finally reaches the Shui

A similar breakthrough occurred among the Shui people. The early missionaries had been unsuccessful in their efforts to establish churches among the Shui, but in 2001 an American Christian shared:

> There are very few Christians among this group, but God is now working among them in great power. From the onset we witnessed many miraculous healings which resulted in numerous salvations . . .
>
> We asked one of the Shui brothers if his wife was saved. He said that she had only become a Christian recently. Many times he had told her of the love of God and how Christ had died for mankind to rescue them from sin, but she had refused to believe.
>
> One day, he and some other believers prayed for a disabled friend who had been crippled since birth. He rose to his feet

and walked for the first time in his life! As a result, our brother's wife was saved. Jesus Christ is alive and well in China. He is revealing Himself to people in real and living ways. The demonstration of God's power through the Holy Spirit is what will convince a dying and lost world to believe.[11]

The kingdom of God continued to expand among the Shui people after Christians helped construct a school for their community. This gesture was so appreciated by the local people that they opened their homes and their hearts to the believers and their message of eternal life. In a short space of time, 150 Shui people placed their trust in Jesus Christ!

The Church among the Shui continued to grow, with house church evangelists from eastern China proving especially effective. One believer entered the Shui area and immediately won the locals' respect because of his farming ability. He showed the Shui how to plow more efficiently, which resulted in increased crop yields. The evangelist refused to be paid for his advice, and said he would be content if the people gave him a place to sleep and daily food. His humble attitude and loving heart attracted many to the gospel, and as a result most of the people in three Shui villages believed in Jesus.

In 2001, a letter from Guizhou shed more light on the impact the house church evangelists were having among the Shui. It said:

> Our church is located in a remote place and transportation is inconvenient. However, the good servants of the Lord have gone to the trouble of traveling a long distance from Zhejiang Province to this impoverished and destitute place where the Shui minority group lives in order to share the gospel with us. The brothers didn't mind climbing mountains and wading across rivers. They got blisters on their feet, but they never complained. In a remote and backward place like Guizhou, they willingly endured hard work and planted many churches.[12]

Today, there are estimated to be approximately 1,000 Shui Christians in Guizhou. Although this number represents a tiny fraction of the half million Shui people, the light has pierced the darkness at long last, and there are strong hopes that the kingdom of God will continue to grow among the Shui as people's lives are transformed by the power of the Holy Spirit.

Massive growth reported

Estimates of the number of Christians in Guizhou were difficult to obtain in the decade from 2000 to 2009. The Three-Self Church appeared to pause its reporting for the decade, perhaps not wanting to alert the national authorities to the true size and scope of Christianity in the province. On the ground, however, it was clear that strong growth was continuing. Many churches were packed out each Sunday, and multitudes of inquirers expressed an insatiable desire to be taught the Word of God.

The respected mission book *Operation World* provided its own analysis of Christian influence in Guizhou, and its figures between the 2001 and 2010 editions of the book reveal a substantial leap in the number of believers. The 2001 edition gave a percentage of Evangelicals in the province that equated to 1.2 million believers,[13] but by the end of the decade their number had more than doubled to nearly 2.6 million Evangelical Christians.[14]

Letters from Guizhou

We conclude this chapter by reprinting a selection of letters that were received from Guizhou by various Christian ministries during the 2000s. These precious communications reveal both the strengths and weaknesses of Christianity in Guizhou, and provide insights into the daily lives and personal struggles of believers as they followed God. Their letters offer a fascinating snapshot of the ever-changing conditions experienced by the body of Christ at this time.

2000

We have just started a Sunday school for children. The Lord has been bringing more and more children to us and we are faced with many practical difficulties, such as the shortage of teaching materials, the teachers' inadequacies, and their lack of experience. All these factors affect the further development of the ministry.[15]

Many young people in our village have been converted, but they are facing opposition and suppression from their families on the grounds that they are forsaking their ancestors because of their Christian belief. A sister woke up one morning and got ready to take a four-hour ride to attend a church with other believers. Her father slapped her on the face several times and would not let her go. In fact, many pagan parents in this village force their converted daughters to marry non-believers so their husbands will have control over them. Some sisters in Christ attempt to escape these forced marriages by finding jobs in the city.[16]

The gospel has spread rapidly in our area over the past several years and the number of saved people has continually increased. However, the church here cannot afford to support their workers. There is a great lack of shepherds and those who serve are not well qualified. In this poor mountain region, the farmers earn so little that they do not even have enough money to buy salt. Since we do not have enough Bible study tools and Christian literature, our needs are not being met. As a result, some believers have been led astray by cults.[17]

2001

After I accepted the Lord I kept looking for churches in my area but could not find any. I heard you teach that someone should be baptized after they accept Jesus Christ, so I told my mother to baptize me. Was what I did okay? I really worry about what I got my mother to do. Please pray for me. I have had a stomach ache for years and I need God's healing touch. I also plan to go to a short-term Bible school.[18]

We have become Christians because of your program. I am 28 years old and have four children. I have always had a short temper, selfish heart, hatred and many other feelings that I cannot control by myself. What should I do to overcome such bad habits? I know that God is able to change my heart but my feelings come back and I explode. What should I do?[19]

Can you help our housewives in the area where I live? Our husbands are crazy about bird-hunting. Even on Sundays they will skip church to go bird-hunting. They go around showcasing the birds they have captured and boast about how beautiful some of them can sing. We women really despise what our husbands and church leaders are doing. Can you give us some advice that will turn our husbands around?[20]

Most of the brothers and sisters in our churches are old and very poor. Some of them eat what they have in one season and cannot store anything for the next. There are even brothers and sisters who are so poor that there is only one pair of trousers in the entire family. I thank the Lord who gave us eternal life, for under the careful nurturing of a good shepherd, our spiritual lives have been gradually improving.[21]

It has been ages since the church workers here had fellowship. They only care about their own ministries; unity doesn't seem to matter. Pastors appoint volunteers to lead fellowship and Bible study groups instead of involving themselves. Worse still, the church workers never care about the effectiveness of the volunteers, the difficulties they face, or their spiritual condition.[22]

A shared opinion among our pastors is that youth ministry is difficult, and we often fail to answer the questions raised by young believers. We lack pastoral advice and counseling on how to put the faith into practice in our daily lives. We generally have problems regarding emotions, marriage, co-habitation, and interpersonal relationships.[23]

2003

The livelihood of Christians among the minority groups is especially poor. These believers often go hungry. Some church workers can't even afford to pay 5 Yuan (US 62 cents) to pay for the bus fare to attend a training session. Instead, they walk for several hours to the center. Worse still, some believers don't have a basic understanding of the truth of God's salvation. Some assume they are born-again at birth because their parents were Christians. As they live in remote mountain regions, it is impossible to obtain the large volumes of resources they need to understand the truth.[24]

Recently, Eastern Lightning cult members have sneaked into some churches. The leaders of these churches are aware of this, and one pastor sent several cult members away in the Name of Jesus Christ. Following that, there were rumors that this pastor had accepted bribes, which caused confusion and split the congregation. Those who are against the pastor are now meeting at another location. Some believers have even left for other churches, while others are caught in the middle, not knowing what to do. Worst of all, the circumstances have caused some believers to stumble and not go to church at all.[25]

2005

After graduation, a theology student returned to the Miao area to pastor a church. Because they are very poor, the church was unable to support the evangelist. The 500 believers decided that each of them would give an annual offering of one Yuan (about US 15 cents) to support him, but after a year, the church could not even raise that amount. Instead, the believers gave their produce to support the evangelist.[26]

A pastor was sent to a mountainous area, where he had to trek nine miles (14 km) to preach. When he arrived at the site, he only found three believers. Afterwards, he walked another nine miles to another hilly area. As the area is remote and no other preacher had gone there before, the people had a great thirst for truth, so when the pastor arrived he was kept by the enthusiastic believers for two hours of worship. He preached for another two hours before the crowd grudgingly let him go.

The pastor had spent the whole day going from one hill to another; he also slept in the mountains at night. There were many fleas and unknown insects. Later in the year he was often tired and had no appetite. His digestive system was ruined and he has frequently been admitted to hospital.[27]

2006

One of our sisters in the Lord has opened a supermarket in Guizhou and has gained certain influence there. While running her business, she also spreads the gospel. She has already set up a number of meeting points at her supermarket and several other places nearby, which serve a total congregation of more than 100 people. Our major mission is to provide training for fellow Christian workers, to help them solve difficulties in their lives, and to supply them with rich spiritual resources.[28]

2009

We are an ethnic minority church with a congregation of 600 mostly elderly believers. Our workers have had little training, and therefore face difficulties in doing pastoral work and teaching the Bible. There is also much room for improvement in our church management. We greatly need Bible teaching in order to train believers who have a low level of education. Our workers also need to be equipped with more Bible knowledge. Please pray for us.[29]

Our church does not have a sound system. During Sunday services, people sitting at the back cannot hear what is said from the pulpit. Gradually, some believers have preferred to stay home or have worked in the fields rather than walking 2–3 hours to attend the service. The pastor is sad to see their weak spiritual lives and feels indebted to God. Please pray for us. May the Lord provide a basic sound system for our congregation of about 2,000 people.[30]

The Dong

The Dong ethnic minority group, which today numbers more than 1.6 million people throughout Guizhou Province, has long been considered difficult to reach with the gospel. Although they have lived alongside the Hmu for many centuries, the Dong are a totally different people and they generally look down on the Hmu and other Miao tribes.

The Dong are concentrated in east and southeast Guizhou. Significant populations of Dong people are also found in the neighboring provinces of Hunan (840,000), Guangxi (300,000) and Hubei (70,000).

A Dong family and their pig in southeast Guizhou
Grigovan/Shutterstock

The Dong are renowned for their unique and skillful architecture and their elaborate festivals, which in recent decades have attracted hordes of tourists, both foreign and domestic, to their villages. The famous Dong drum towers and "wind and rain" bridges have intrigued international architects, who have come to study the fascinating designs.

Little interest in the gospel

Evangelical work among the Dong began when CIM missionaries visited the area in the 1880s. Being unable to speak their language, the handful of workers made little or no headway. Although the Dong were friendly, few showed any interest in the message of eternal life.

Despite being such a large and influential group, the Dong were not a major target for outreach for many years. Finally,

The unique architecture of a Dong village in southern Guizhou
IMB

in the 1930s a new strategy was implemented to reach them. Missionaries based at Liuzhou in Guangxi Province traveled north and won 80 Dong people to faith in Christ at Fulu, on the Guangxi–Guizhou border.

After all foreign missionaries were expelled from China in the early 1950s, nothing more was heard about the Dong believers, and it was assumed that most or all of them had fallen away from the faith during the harsh persecutions. Years later, however, news emerged that many Dong people had turned to Christ in neighboring Guangxi.

In the summer of 1957, a surprise appeal was received by a church in the city of Nanning for workers to go to the Dong. A three-day journey brought the Chinese believers to a remote mountainous area. After some time:

> a total of 433 persons from 16 villages were baptized and a
> church was set up. Some of these people had been waiting for

A traditional Dong "wind and rain bridge" in southern Guizhou
IMB

12 years for baptism. One of the first believers was a woman in her 50s and among those baptized were several white-haired old men.[1]

A Holy Spirit-inspired dream

The overwhelming majority of Dong people in Guizhou were still completely unevangelized during the 1990s, most never having even heard the name of Jesus Christ. Things began to change after a pastor in the United States had a strange dream in 1997.

In the dream, Ron Johnson of the Bethel Temple in Hampton, Virginia, saw himself sitting with some others in a four-wheel-drive vehicle, driving down a dirt road toward a river. As they drew closer to the river he saw a large wooden bridge with tall towers spaced evenly from one end to the other. In the dream he stopped and spoke with a local man, who said to Johnson, "Pastor, you are to lead an outreach to this place."

The dream was so vivid that Johnson couldn't get it out of his mind. He had never been to Asia before, but in his heart he felt the bridge was somewhere in China. Johnson assigned his mission director to try to discover where such a bridge was located.

Unknown to the pastor and mission leader, a man named Gary Klein had just returned from China a few months earlier and had started attending the church. He arranged a meeting with Johnson, as he intended to challenge the church to consider working among the unreached minority groups of China. Johnson interrupted Klein and told him about the strange bridge he had seen in his dream. Klein raced out to his car and retrieved a video on China's unreached people groups, and played it to the pastor. The first scene in the video was of a traditional Dong bridge with large towers. "That's the bridge in my dream!" the pastor excitedly exclaimed.

The Virginia church connected with some foreign missionaries, and teams of intercessors and evangelists began visiting the Dong region. God worked quickly, and in 1998 several Dong people were led to Jesus Christ during a short visit. The new believers returned to their village and established a house fellowship which quickly grew to 40 people.

By 2002, more than 20 evangelists had been trained and sent to share the gospel among unreached Dong communities. Relief work also commenced, with medical clinics providing free treatment to many afflicted people. All of these outreaches demonstrated the love of God, opening the hearts of many Dong people to the claims of the gospel.

An elderly Dong man taking a rest
IMB

Christianity among the Dong today

Since 1997, when the American pastor Ron Johnson received a dream from God, the kingdom of God has continued to advance among the Dong people of Guizhou. Since that time, Christians both from overseas and from Chinese house church networks have lovingly labored among the Dong. The *Jesus* film was produced, followed by the New Testament which was translated into Southern Dong in 2006.[2]

A mission group visited the Dong at regular intervals, following up on the seed that was sown. In 2009, one of the workers reported, "We are seeing growth in all areas of our work. Among the Dong, 14 churches have now been planted, and more leadership training is going on."[3]

By 2013 the missionaries seemed satisfied that their work among the Dong was now advancing under its own steam, and they began to refocus their efforts on other unreached people groups in China. A ministry leader wrote:

> Our April trip was a success. We were able to send out 15 Dong evangelists to new areas, and they have already sent word that there is a great openness in these new outreach areas, with people coming to Christ.
>
> One of our Dong churches is growing so fast that they dug out a basement in their home and it filled with people the first Sunday they met. Pray this Dong church will multiply and affect everyone around them with the love of Christ. To God be the glory![4]

The gospel has continued to expand slowly, and today an estimated 3,000 Dong people profess Jesus Christ as Lord, although this number represents only a tiny portion of the large and widespread Dong population.

Finally, after God had patiently waited more than a century as generations of Dong people died without any knowledge of

His beloved Son, a powerful work was underway among the Dong. It is hoped that many more thousands of Dong people will soon experience God's life-changing gift of salvation, and that the gospel may also spread to the many other unreached people groups in eastern Guizhou.

2010s

The Church pushes back

The first half of the decade between 2010 and 2015 proved relatively calm for the Church in Guizhou. God's kingdom continued to advance, with many believers being established in the faith and remote districts hearing the gospel for the first time.

Despite the peaceful interlude, cruel persecution occasionally broke out in the province. At Bijie in 2013, a Christian Miao woman named Li Fengfei was forced by government officials to have a second trimester abortion. The procedure not only killed her precious baby, but also left Li in critical condition.

Li Fengfei
China Aid

In the age of social media, she took to the internet to share her story of abuse. In response, the Jinsha Municipal Public Security Bureau brought trumped-up charges and arrested her for embezzlement.

As another sign of the times, a Guiyang legal firm, led by a Christian lawyer named Li Guisheng, met with Li Fengfei in prison and took on her case against the corrupt government. They found that she had previously held an important job as an accountant at a Bijie bank, but when the bank manager wanted to embezzle money, Li Fengfei refused to falsify the documents as it was contrary to her faith in Jesus Christ. This righteous stand was the origin of the false charges brought against her. The bank manager had family members who worked in the county's Communist disciplinary committee, and they framed Li in a bid to hide their own evil deeds.[1]

Sister Li's horrible account is just one of countless similar experiences that Christian women have been made to endure throughout Guizhou and the rest of China. Thousands of women have been forcibly sterilized to prevent them having children, and a long roll of misery has been inflicted upon the children of light by the God-hating atheists who control the reins of power in China.

In recent years, many Christians have adopted a new approach in response to persecution and harassment by government officials. In 2014, after 12 house church Christians were arrested for possessing a hymnal which the government deemed illegal, five of the detained believers filed administrative lawsuits to challenge their arrests.[2]

Despite this new approach by some Christians, persecution continued to be a reality in the lives of many believers in Guizhou. In the town of Daguan, dozens of armed police officers with attack dogs raided a Sunday worship service on June 1, 2015, arresting dozens of the 70 to 80 believers gathered for the service. The officers released their savage dogs on the congregation, most of whom were impoverished farmers. Many people were bitten, and all the believers' possessions were confiscated, despite the failure of the police to produce any search warrant or reason to conduct the raid.[3]

Several weeks after the incident, 11 Daguan Christians remained in custody. It transpired that the local government officials were alarmed by the large numbers of people becoming Christians, and they had threatened to cut off government assistance to anyone who converted to Christianity. Many people who had joyfully found Jesus Christ firmly resisted the

A Three-Self church attended by Miao Christians
Miao Messenger

threats. The officials launched their raid in retaliation, but it did nothing to dim the believers' zeal. Instead, it made them even more determined to follow God wholeheartedly and to share the gospel with unbelievers.

Many similar incidents have marked a new line in the sand for Christian leaders in Guizhou. At times, the authorities appeared bewildered by the aggressive legal pushback from Christians, who were fed up with being abused by corrupt officials. The believers, for their part, stressed that their trust is in the Lord Jesus for deliverance. For decades they had suffered in silence, but encouraged by the apostle Paul's occasional use of his legal rights when he preached the gospel, the Guizhou Christians decided to fight back, first in prayer, but also through China's developing legal system.

2016—a storm is unleashed

In 2016, China dramatically reversed its policies, and full-scale persecution of house church Christians broke out in many parts of the country, including Guizhou. The directive to crush the house churches appears to have come directly from the Chinese president Xi Jinping, who urged action against Christians in several speeches. New laws had been quickly passed in 2015 to help implement the furious storm that was about to be unleashed against the body of Christ throughout China.

Pressure was placed on Guizhou's Christians in various ways. At Huaqiu, government officials threatened believers and tried to intimidate them by punishing their children. After issuing an official notice:

> Government personnel coerced members of the Huaqiu Church to sign a document saying they would no longer take minors to church. Any children who attend the church will be ineligible

for the college entrance exam or admittance into a military academy, and parents who continue to bring their children to church will be sued.[4]

House church leaders were the main target of the government crackdown. They were ordered to register their congregations with the Three-Self Patriotic Movement, and to provide the full names and details of every person who attended their services. When they refused to do so, many pastors were arrested and forced to endure barbaric torture. When the believers at Huaqiu refused to submit to the bullying, the authorities seized the property and demolished their church building, citing an obscure building code violation.

The wide-ranging crackdown on Christians occurred even in remote tribal areas of Guizhou, with one minister of the gospel reporting in November 2016:

> In the past few months, new regulations in China have been put into effect to persecute believers. Christians in Miao areas have been followed, questioned, falsely accused, imprisoned, chased from the towns where they live, and denied basic rights that most citizens enjoy, such as pensions for the elderly and college education.[5]

The Huoshi Church

After receiving new directives to destroy the house churches, the authorities in Guizhou wasted little time. They targeted the Huoshi ("Living Stone") Church, which had quickly grown to become the largest house church in Guiyang, with a congregation of about 700 believers. The main leader of the church, Li Guozhi, is commonly known by his spiritual pseudonym Yang Hua.

The trouble started for Yang in 2015, when he was arrested along with other pastors and deacons of the Huoshi Church.

Pastor Yang Hua
www.freeyanghua.org

The congregation had outgrown their facilities at the time, so they purchased office space on the twenty-fourth floor of the Huaguoyuan International Center in Guiyang, and began to hold their services there. Government officials heard about their plans and warned them not to proceed, and issued a threat that all attendees would be arrested. Yang and his co-leaders refused to bow to the intimidation, and they held an opening dedication service, which was attended by hundreds of believers.

On October 21, 2015, the authorities carried out their threats. A notice was posted stating that the church was an illegal gathering, and that none of its leaders were ordained religious practitioners approved by the state. A cumulative fine was put into effect, with the church required to pay 12,960 Yuan (more than $2,000) per day until it was closed down.

When the church leaders still refused to comply with the orders, officers were dispatched to disrupt the meetings on numerous occasions. Believers were harassed and filmed, property was confiscated, and some church members were arrested.

Yang was also arrested, and was beaten and tortured in detention, before a black hood was placed over his head and he was moved in an unlicensed vehicle to a different facility to await trial.

The Huoshi Church had functioned in a way that Chinese believers of previous generations could never have fathomed. The congregation consisted of believers from all walks of life, including wealthy businesspeople and humble street-sweepers. They had legally purchased the facility and were paying off a monthly mortgage of 30,000 Yuan ($4,500) when the arrests occurred. The government banned their meetings and froze the church's bank account, which contained a balance of 600,000 Yuan ($88,000) at the time. This prevented the church from meeting its mortgage obligations.

In January 2016, the severity of Yang's case was greatly increased after the corrupt government officials altered the charges against the unassuming pastor to "divulging state secrets," a serious charge that potentially carries the death penalty.

The Huoshi church members banded together and secured legal counsel to fight the charges, and a website was created to update concerned Christians in China and around the world of the plight of the pastor and his scattered congregation. The case quickly grew in prominence as alarmed church leaders throughout China realized that Yang's arrest was likely to set a new precedent, and that if he was charged as a spy, then similar charges could be leveled against other pastors throughout the country.

On June 30, 2016, Yang Hua wrote a loving letter from prison to his wife, detailing some of the methods used against him to extract a forced confession. He also courageously shared some of the spiritual benefits his incarceration had produced:

> This is a good place to rest, where I am cut off from the rest of the world and brought closer to God. I can no longer hear the clamorous noises, but can better listen to the Lord's still voice . . . Genuine rest has nothing to do with the environment. No matter if the waves are quiet or the sea roars, our hearts rest in God as a weaned child sleeps in its mother's arms. I want to thank God for using this special method to give this gift to our family. Let us accept and enjoy it with thankful hearts.[6]

In January 2017, after more than a year in custody, Yang Hua was finally convicted on the spurious charge of divulging state secrets and was sentenced to two and a half years in prison. The same men who had tortured Yang in prison were allowed to act as the court prosecutors.

The Huoshi Church, meanwhile, struggled to reorganize itself after the savage persecution, but the government, as always, failed to comprehend that the kingdom of God lives in the hearts of believers, so that even if their bodies are killed the living seed of God's Word goes on achieving His eternal purposes. The Huoshi believers began meeting in smaller home groups, and the praises of Jesus Christ continued to rise up to heaven.

By October 2017, all hope of justice seemed to have died for Yang Hua. As he continued to languish behind bars in Kaili Prison, the government fined him and another church leader, Su Tianfu, the exorbitant sum of 7 million Yuan (just over $1 million), which officials claimed the church had received as "illegal income" between 2009 and 2015. The two pastors applied to the legal system to argue that it was the church's income, not their own, and that as the church expenses during those six years had exceeded the income, there was no case to be answered. Their request for a hearing was denied.

The fire still burns among the tribes

While the house churches in many parts of Guizhou were under intense pressure from the new and sustained government crackdown, the gospel continued to advance among the people groups in the province, one transformed life at a time.

The Horned Miao—so called because of the women's custom of wearing wooden horns on their heads—boast a population

A large group of Christians from the Horned Miao tribe meet on a hillside in Guizhou
OMF

of approximately 80,000 people, distributed throughout 550 villages in Guizhou.

Although they live in the same general area as the A-Hmao and Gha-Mu tribes, both of which have contained thousands of Christians for over a century, the Horned Miao have only recently experienced a widespread turning to Jesus Christ.

The movement began in 2004, and grew exponentially after Horned Miao church leaders received Bible training. They took the fire from the altar of God and launched an initiative to plant churches in all 550 Horned Miao villages within three years.

The leaders were true to their commitment, and empowered by the Holy Spirit, thousands of Horned Miao people met Christ for the first time. As the movement expanded, the new churches soon faced the same challenges that countless other tribes had encountered before them. Almost all Horned Miao people are illiterate, and no Bible portions or Scripture

A Miao congregation at Ziyun, Guizhou
China Christian Daily

recordings exist in their language. The church leaders faced the difficult task of establishing believers in sound doctrine without any part of the Bible being available in their heart language.

In recent years, news emerged that another strong Christian movement had occurred among the Hmong Shua tribe, who first heard the gospel from James Adam more than a century ago. Many new Hmong Shua churches containing hundreds of Christians were established, and a Bible translation project in the Hmong Shua language was launched. Bible stories were produced in audio form, and work commenced to translate the *Jesus* film into Hmong Shua.

After decades of slow progress with little to show for the efforts of the early pioneer missionaries, the kingdom of God was finally flourishing among these two tribes and others throughout Guizhou.

The future of the Church in Guizhou

As we reach the end of our look at the wonderful things God has done in Guizhou Province, one thing is clear: despite decades of battering and persecution, the Lord Jesus Christ has raised up a vibrant body of believers from among Guizhou's population of 35 million people.

The early Evangelical missionaries in the nineteenth century overcame overwhelming obstacles to plant the seed of the gospel in the province. The first pioneers in Guizhou expected to see a strong response from the Han Chinese, but they were surprised to find resistance to their message from the majority people. Instead, they found fertile soil in the hearts of some of Guizhou's poor ethnic minority groups, and a mighty revival broke out among the A-Hmao, Gha-Mu and several other Miao tribes.

And what a revival it was! The Holy Spirit moved on thousands of people, causing them to press eagerly into the kingdom of God. Two Scottish missionaries, James Adam and Samuel Pollard, emerged as key figures in the work.

The adage "Success breeds success" can also be applied in the mission world, and the majority of new missionaries in Guizhou were sent to help sustain the exciting revival among the Miao. This allocation of workers and resources created a lopsided situation in the province. Many Han Chinese were baffled as to why the foreign missionaries focused so much on the Miao, whom they had despised for centuries.

An unexpected dichotomy emerged. Thousands of tribal people were being baptized each year, but for decades the Han Chinese and many other ethnic groups remained comparatively untouched by the gospel. Even today, many Han people in Guizhou dismiss Christianity as "the Miao religion."

After Adam and Pollard unexpectedly died, the tribal work suffered a temporary setback, but the Lord had laid a deep foundation in the hearts of His children, and before long the churches were flourishing again. As the leadership of the Church gradually passed from foreign to local control, it matured and strengthened into a powerful remnant that was able to withstand decades of hardship.

The 1950s to 1980s marked a terrible time for Christians in Guizhou, with many being martyred for their faith in Jesus. When the long and bitter winter began to draw to a close, a new era of openness in the 1990s revealed that not only had Christianity survived the storm, but God's family had actually grown in many areas, and new tribes that had previously been difficult to reach were now receptive to the gospel, including the Nosu tribes.

The last 30 years also saw a new wave of foreign missionaries serving throughout Guizhou. They didn't come as official missionaries but adopted a variety of different roles, working as teachers, students, investors or researchers. God blessed their efforts, and after the house church networks from other parts of China received a burden for Guizhou, many evangelists were sent to engage the unreached peoples in the province.

The deep racial hatred and resentment that existed between the Han and the Miao for centuries has gradually eroded. While suspicion and bitterness still exists in some rural areas today, the Han have gradually come to appreciate rather than mock the cultural richness of Guizhou's minority groups, while new generations of tribal people have slowly come to accept their position in the modern China.

Since the start of the new millennium, significant breakthroughs have taken place among minority groups that had been ignored for generations. There are growing churches today among minority groups like the Dong, Shui and, to a lesser extent, the Bouyei. The mighty revival among the Han Chinese that has spread throughout China over the past 40 years has also impacted many Chinese in Guizhou, while some of the partially assimilated, Mandarin-speaking minority groups (such as the Gelao and Tujia) have also benefited from the overflow of spiritual blessing from the Holy Spirit's visitation.

Finally, after 130 years of agonizing struggle, the Church among the Han Chinese also began to flourish in Guizhou and has grown rapidly. As the subsequent tables and maps in the Appendix of this book reveal, we estimate there to be approximately 2.7 million professing Christians in Guizhou Province today. Of these, about 1.5 million belong to unregistered Evangelical house churches, 900,000 attend government-approved Three-Self churches, while Catholics—despite enjoying a head start of more than a century over their Protestant counterparts—today number approximately 270,000 adherents in the province.

As our "People groups in Guizhou" table reveals, dozens of small tribes remain isolated from the good news, with many groups containing no known Christians at the present time. Perhaps the most urgent need for the gospel is among the two dozen Miao tribes that remain unevangelized. These distinct peoples have been grouped according to their linguistic affiliations, with several clustered together to form each of the Guiyang, Huishui, and Mashan Miao peoples. These unreached tribes continue to live as they have lived for centuries, going about their daily tasks without the slightest knowledge of Jesus Christ.

The Hmu remain the largest unreached people group in Guizhou. The history of Christian work among them has been traumatic, and right at the moment when many seemed to be on the verge of turning to Christ, a mass murder of believers caused the Hmu to recoil from the gospel. Their reluctance to embrace Christianity has tragically continued for more than a century to the present time. Much intercessory prayer and loving outreach will be required to break the spirit of fear and resistance that has built up among the precious Hmu people over a century.

In previous generations, Guizhou's Christians faced famine, bandits, disease and war. Today they are battling materialism, cults, and a central government that once again appears determined in its desire to obliterate Christianity. Over the years, many professing believers in Guizhou have struggled without a strong spiritual foundation, exacerbated by the lack of Bibles and a dire shortage of trained church leaders.

Although there is much to rejoice about when we consider the marvelous deeds that God has performed in Guizhou, it is sobering to realize that today less than 8 percent of the population professes to be Christian. This means that 92 out of every 100 people have yet to believe in Jesus Christ, and millions have yet to hear the gospel in any meaningful manner that would enable them to accept or reject God's offer of salvation.

For all the good reports of what God has done in Guizhou, much more remains to be done before the Lamb of God will receive His full reward from among the peoples of China's Precious Province.

Appendix

Evangelical Christians in Guizhou (1877–2020)

(Both Three-Self and house churches)

1877 0

1893 |70

1904 |123

1922 ▮ 20,873

1949 |10,000

1987 ▮ 100,000

1993 ▮▮▮ 350,000

1997 ▮▮▮ 400,000

1999 ▮▮▮ 500,000

2001 ▮▮▮▮▮▮▮ 1,221,000

2010 ▮▮▮▮▮▮▮▮▮▮▮▮▮▮▮ 2,592,600

2020 ▮▮▮▮▮▮▮▮▮▮▮▮▮▮ 2,429,000

0	0.5	1	1.5	2	2.5	3

Millions

Appendix

Sources:

0	(1877)
70	(1893 – *China Mission Handbook*, 1896)
123	(1904 – *China's Millions*, November 1905)
20,873	(1922 – Stauffer, *The Christian Occupation of China*)
10,000	(1949 – *Bridge*, July–August 1987)
100,000	(1987 – *Bridge*, July–August 1987)*
350,000	(1993 – Lambert, *The Resurrection of the Chinese Church*)*
400,000	(1997 – Lambert, personal communication)*
500,000	(1999 – Intercessors for China)
1,221,000	(2001 – Johnstone and Mandryk, *Operation World*)
2,592,600	(2010 – Mandryk, *Operation World*)
2,429,000	(2020 – Hattaway, the China Chronicles)

* These sources may only refer to registered church estimates. Three-Self figures typically only count adult baptized members.

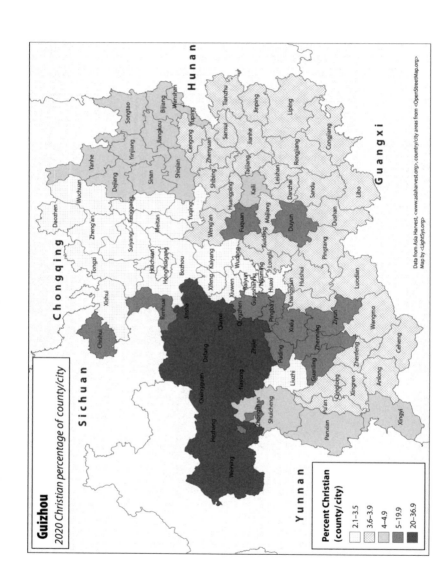

Guizhou

2020 Christian percentage of county/city

S i c h u a n

C h o n g q i n g

H u n a n

G u a n g x i

Y u n n a n

Percent Christian (county/city)

- 2.1–3.5
- 3.6–3.9
- 4–4.9
- 5–19.9
- 20–36.9

Data from Asia Harvest, <www.asiaharvest.org>, country/city areas from <OpenStreetMap.org>
Map by <Light5ys.org>

China *Christian percentage of county/city*

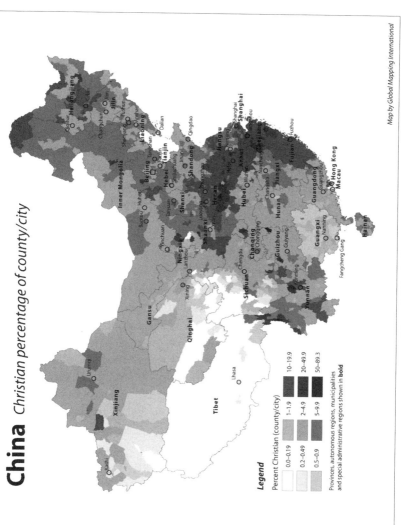

Legend

Percent Christian (county/city)

- 0.0–0.19
- 0.2–0.49
- 0.5–0.9
- 1–1.9
- 2–4.9
- 5–9.9
- 10–19.9
- 20–49.9
- 50–89.3

Provinces, autonomous regions, municipalities
and special administrative regions shown in **bold**

Map by Global Mapping International

Map of China's Christians

A survey of Christians in China

For centuries, people have been curious to know how many Christians live in China. When Marco Polo made his famous journey to the Orient 700 years ago, he revealed the existence of Nestorian churches and monasteries in various places, to the fascination of people back in Europe.

Since I started traveling to China in the 1980s, I have found that Christians around the world are still eager to know how many believers there are in China. Many people are aware that God has done a remarkable work in the world's most populated country, but little research has been done to put a figure on this phenomenon. In recent decades, wildly divergent estimates have been published, ranging from 20 million to 230 million Christians in China.

Methodology

In the table on pages 233–5, I provide estimates of the number of Christians in Guizhou. Full tables of the other provinces of China can be found at the Asia Harvest website (see the "The Church in China" link under the Resources tab at <www.asiaharvest.org>). My survey provides figures for Christians of every creed, arranged in four main categories: the Three-Self Patriotic Movement; the Evangelical house churches; the Catholic Patriotic Association; and the Catholic house churches. I have supplied statistics for all 2,370 cities and counties within every province, municipality and autonomous region of China.

The information was gathered from a wide variety of sources. More than 2,000 published sources have been noted in the tables published online, including a multitude of books, journals, magazine articles and reports that I spent years meticulously accumulating. I have also conducted hundreds of hours of interviews with key house church leaders responsible for their church networks throughout China.

Before entering data into the tables, I began with this assumption: that in any given place in China there are no Christians at all, until I have a figure from a documented source or can make an intelligent estimate based on information gathered from Chinese Christian leaders. In other words, I wanted to put aside all preconceptions and expectations, input all the information I had, and see what the totals came to.

A note about security

None of the information provided in these tables is new to the Chinese government. Beijing has already thoroughly researched the spread of Christianity throughout the country, as shown by high-ranking official Ye Xiaowen's 2006 announcement that there were then 130 million Christians in China. In December 2009, the national newspaper *China Daily* interviewed scholar Liu Peng who had spent years researching religion for the Chinese Academy of Social Sciences. Liu claimed the "house churches have at least 50 million followers nationwide." His figure at the time was consistent with my research.

After consulting various house church leaders in China, I was able to confirm that all of them were content that this information should be published, as long as the surveys focus on statistics and avoid specific information such as the names and locations of Christian leaders.

The Chinese Church in perspective

All discussion of how many Christians there are in China today should be tempered by the realization that more than 90 percent of the population faces a Christless eternity. Hundreds of millions of individuals have yet to hear the gospel. Church leaders in China have told me how ashamed and burdened they feel that so many of their countrymen and women do not yet know Jesus Christ. This burden motivates them to do whatever it takes to preach the gospel among every ethnic group and in every city, town and village—to every individual—in China, and to do whatever necessary to see Christ exalted throughout the land.

May we humbly give thanks to the living God for the great things He has done in China. We are privileged to live in a remarkable time in human history, like in the days prophesied by the prophet Habakkuk:

> Look at the nations and watch—and be utterly amazed. For I am going to do something in your days that you would not believe, even if you were told.
>
> (Habakkuk 1.5)

Table of Christians in Guizhou

| Guizhou 贵州 | POPULATION | | | | | CHRISTIANS | | | | | | | Total Christians | |
| | | | | | | Evangelicals | | | Catholics | | | | | |
Location	Census 2000	Census 2010	Growth	Growth (percent)	Estimate 2020	TSPM	House church	TOTAL Evangelicals	CPA	House church	TOTAL Catholics	TOTAL	Percent of 2020 population
Anshun Prefecture 安顺市													
Guanling County 关岭布依族苗族自治县	280,755	301,363	20,608	7.34	321,971	8,403	14,566	22,969	795	1,591	2,386	25,355	7.87
Pingba District 平坝区	323,959	297,990	-25,969	-8.02	272,021	7,100	12,306	19,406	672	1,344	2,016	21,421	7.87
Puding County 普定县	353,803	378,452	24,649	6.97	403,101	10,521	18,236	28,757	996	1,991	2,987	31,744	7.87
Xixiu District 西秀区	767,307	765,399	-1,908	-0.25	763,491	19,922	34,540	54,467	1,886	3,772	5,657	60,124	7.87
Zhenning County 镇宁布依族苗族自治县	308,569	284,063	-24,506	-7.94	259,557	6,774	11,742	18,517	641	1,282	1,923	20,440	7.87
Ziyun County 紫云苗族布依族自治县	297,348	270,345	-27,003	-9.08	243,342	6,351	11,009	17,360	601	1,202	1,803	19,163	7.87
	2,331,741	2,297,612	-34,129	-1.46	2,263,483	59,077	102,398	161,475	5,591	11,182	16,772	178,247	7.87
Bijie Prefecture 毕节市													
Dafang County 大方县	851,729	776,324	-75,405	-8.85	700,919	92,521	160,367	252,888	1,731	3,463	5,194	258,082	36.82
Hezhang County 赫章县	611,243	649,357	38,114	6.24	687,471	56,373	97,711	154,083	1,698	3,396	5,094	159,177	23.15
Jinsha County 金沙县	496,063	560,575	64,512	13.00	625,087	51,257	88,844	140,101	1,544	3,088	4,632	144,733	23.15
Nayong County 纳雍县	661,772	670,272	8,500	1.28	678,772	55,659	96,474	152,134	1,677	3,353	5,030	157,163	23.15
Qianxi County 黔西县	697,075	695,947	-1,128	-0.16	694,819	56,975	98,755	155,730	1,716	3,432	5,149	160,879	23.15
Qixingguan District 七星关区	1,128,230	1,137,383	9,153	0.81	1,146,536	94,016	162,958	256,974	2,832	5,664	8,496	265,470	23.15
Weining County 威宁彝族回族苗族自治县	1,056,009	1,263,521	207,512	19.65	1,471,033	120,625	209,079	329,704	3,633	7,267	10,900	340,604	23.15
Zhijin County 织金县	825,350	784,119	-41,231	-5.00	742,888	60,917	105,587	166,504	1,835	3,670	5,505	172,009	23.15
	6,327,471	6,537,498	210,027	3.32	6,747,525	588,343	1,019,775	1,608,118	16,666	33,333	49,999	1,658,117	24.57
Guiyang Prefecture 贵阳市													
Baiyun District 白云区	187,695	264,496	76,801	40.92	341,297	2,770	4,801	7,571	1,399	2,799	4,198	11,769	3.45
Guanshanhu District 观山湖区	167,256	167,256	0	0.00	167,256	1,357	2,353	3,710	686	1,371	2,057	5,768	3.45
Huaxi District 花溪区	480,164	607,051	126,887	26.43	733,938	5,957	10,325	16,281	3,009	6,018	9,027	25,309	3.45
Kaiyang County 开阳县	389,252	358,248	-31,004	-7.97	327,244	2,656	4,603	7,259	1,342	2,683	4,025	11,285	3.45
Nanming District 南明区	687,804	829,326	141,522	20.58	970,848	7,879	13,657	21,537	3,980	7,961	11,941	33,478	3.45
Qingzhen City 清镇市	471,305	467,790	-3,515	-0.75	464,275	8,821	15,290	24,111	1,904	3,807	5,711	29,822	6.42
Wudang District 乌当区	209,715	209,715	0	0.00	209,715	1,702	2,950	4,652	860	1,720	2,579	7,232	3.45
Xifeng County 息烽县	221,583	212,897	-8,686	-3.92	204,211	1,657	2,873	4,530	837	1,675	2,512	7,042	3.45
Xiuwen County 修文县	262,039	248,926	-13,113	-5.00	235,813	1,914	3,317	5,231	967	1,934	2,900	8,132	3.45
Yunyan District 云岩区	698,988	956,906	257,918	36.90	1,214,824	9,860	17,089	26,949	4,981	9,962	14,942	41,891	3.45
	3,718,449	4,322,611	546,810	14.71	4,869,421	44,573	77,259	121,832	19,965	39,929	59,894	181,726	3.73
Liupanshui Prefecture 六盘水市													
Liuzhi District 六枝特区	541,762	495,162	-46,600	-8.60	448,562	2,243	3,887	6,130	1,108	2,216	3,324	9,454	2.11
Pan County 盘县	1,070,802	1,035,345	-35,457	-3.31	999,888	15,098	26,170	41,268	2,470	4,939	7,409	48,677	4.87
Shuicheng County 水城县	678,228	704,615	26,387	3.89	731,002	11,111	19,259	30,370	1,806	3,611	5,417	35,787	4.90
Zhongshan District 钟山区	453,293	616,210	162,917	35.94	779,127	20,959	36,327	57,286	1,924	3,849	5,773	63,059	8.09
	2,744,085	2,851,332	107,247	3.91	2,958,579	49,411	85,644	135,055	7,308	14,615	21,923	156,978	5.31

| Guizhou 贵州 | POPULATION | | | | | CHRISTIANS | | | | | | | |
| | | | | | | Evangelicals | | | Catholics | | | Total Christians | |
Location	Census 2000	Census 2010	Growth	Growth (percent)	Estimate 2020	TSPM	House church	TOTAL Evangelicals	CPA	House church	TOTAL Catholics	TOTAL	Percent of 2020 population
Qiandongnan Prefecture 黔东南苗族侗族自治州													
Cengong County 岑巩县	187,734	162,444	-25,290	-13.47	137,154	1,564	2,710	4,274	339	678	1,016	5,290	3.86
Congjiang County 从江县	301,513	290,960	-10,553	-3.50	280,407	3,197	5,541	8,737	693	1,385	2,078	10,815	3.86
Danzhai County 丹寨县	135,400	122,430	-12,970	-9.58	109,460	1,248	2,163	3,411	270	541	811	4,222	3.86
Huangping County 黄平县	292,121	263,363	-28,758	-9.84	234,605	2,674	4,636	7,310	579	1,159	1,738	9,049	3.86
Jianhe County 剑河县	189,085	180,624	-8,461	-4.47	172,163	1,963	3,402	5,365	425	850	1,276	6,640	3.86
Jinping County 锦屏县	190,429	154,869	-35,560	-18.67	119,309	1,360	2,358	3,718	295	589	884	4,602	3.86
Kaili City 凯里市	433,236	479,011	45,775	10.57	524,786	7,347	12,735	20,082	1,296	2,592	3,889	23,970	4.57
Leishan County 雷山县	132,004	117,190	-14,814	-11.22	102,376	1,167	2,023	3,190	253	506	759	3,949	3.86
Liping County 黎平县	458,533	391,047	-67,486	-14.72	323,561	3,689	6,393	10,082	799	1,598	2,398	12,480	3.86
Majiang County 麻江县	203,481	167,641	-35,840	-17.61	131,801	1,503	2,604	4,107	326	651	977	5,084	3.86
Rongjiang County 榕江县	300,369	286,322	-14,047	-4.68	272,275	3,104	5,380	8,484	673	1,345	2,018	10,502	3.86
Sansui County 三穗县	170,167	155,735	-14,432	-8.48	141,303	1,611	2,792	4,403	349	698	1,047	5,450	3.86
Shibing County 施秉县	137,171	130,464	-6,707	-4.89	123,757	1,411	2,445	3,856	306	611	917	4,773	3.86
Taijiang County 台江县	142,386	112,319	-30,067	-21.12	82,252	938	1,625	2,563	203	406	609	3,172	3.86
Tianzhu County 天柱县	348,302	263,850	-84,452	-24.25	179,398	2,045	3,545	5,590	443	886	1,329	6,919	3.86
Zhenyuan County 镇远县	222,766	203,622	-19,144	-8.59	184,478	2,103	3,645	5,748	456	911	1,367	7,115	3.86
Qiandongnan Prefecture 黔东南苗族侗族自治州	3,844,697	3,481,891	-362,806	-9.44	3,119,085	36,922	63,997	100,919	7,704	15,408	23,112	124,031	3.86
Qiannan Prefecture 黔南布依族苗族自治州													
Changshun County 长顺县	226,235	191,129	-35,106	-15.52	156,023	1,779	3,083	4,862	385	771	1,156	6,018	3.86
Dushan County 独山县	317,910	265,212	-52,698	-16.58	212,514	2,423	4,199	6,622	525	1,050	1,575	8,197	3.86
Duyun City 都匀市	463,426	443,721	-19,705	-4.25	424,016	8,480	14,699	23,179	1,047	2,095	3,142	26,321	6.21
Fuquan City 福泉市	292,720	283,904	-8,816	-3.01	275,088	6,602	11,443	18,046	679	1,359	2,038	20,084	7.30
Guiding County 贵定县	267,809	231,118	-36,691	-13.70	194,427	2,216	3,842	6,058	480	960	1,441	7,499	3.86
Huishui County 惠水县	388,896	342,647	-46,249	-11.89	296,398	3,379	5,857	9,236	732	1,464	2,196	11,432	3.86
Libo County 荔波县	171,366	144,865	-26,501	-15.46	118,364	1,349	2,339	3,688	292	585	877	4,565	3.86
Longli County 龙里县	192,436	180,865	-11,571	-6.01	169,294	1,930	3,345	5,275	418	836	1,254	6,530	3.86
Luodian County 罗甸县	293,994	257,236	-36,758	-12.50	220,478	2,513	4,357	6,870	545	1,089	1,634	8,504	3.86
Pingtang County 平塘县	267,368	228,560	-38,808	-14.51	189,752	2,163	3,749	5,913	469	937	1,406	7,319	3.86
Sandu County 三都水族自治县	297,442	283,139	-14,303	-4.81	268,836	3,065	5,312	8,377	664	1,328	1,992	10,369	3.86
Weng'an County 瓮安县	390,245	380,318	-9,927	-2.54	370,391	4,222	7,319	11,541	915	1,830	2,745	14,286	3.86
Qiannan Prefecture 黔南布依族苗族自治州	3,569,847	3,232,714	-337,133	-9.44	2,895,581	40,122	69,544	109,666	7,152	14,304	21,456	131,122	3.98
Qianxinan Prefecture 黔西南布依族苗族自治州													
Anlong County 安龙县	399,384	356,255	-43,129	-10.80	313,126	3,570	6,187	9,757	773	1,547	2,320	12,077	4.53
Ceheng County 册亨县	215,030	190,413	-24,617	-11.45	165,796	1,890	3,276	5,166	410	819	1,229	6,395	3.86
Pu'an County 普安县	259,881	254,247	-5,634	-2.17	248,613	2,834	4,912	7,747	614	1,228	1,842	9,589	3.86
Qinglong County 晴隆县	258,031	246,809	-11,222	-4.35	235,587	2,686	4,655	7,341	582	1,164	1,746	9,087	3.86
Wangmo County 望谟县	273,113	251,966	-21,147	-7.74	230,819	2,631	4,561	7,192	570	1,140	1,710	8,903	3.86
Xingren County 兴仁县	425,091	417,919	-7,172	-1.69	410,747	4,683	8,116	12,799	1,015	2,029	3,044	15,842	3.86

Guizhou 贵州

Location		POPULATION					CHRISTIANS								
							Evangelicals			Catholics			Total Christians		
		Census 2000	Census 2010	Growth	Growth (percent)	Estimate 2020	TSPM	House church	TOTAL Evangelicals	CPA	House church	TOTAL Catholics	TOTAL	Percent of 2020 population
Qianxinan Prefecture (continued)														
Xingyi City	兴义市	719,605	783,120	63,515	8.83	846,635	10,160	17,610	27,769	2,091	4,182	6,274	34,043	4.02
Zhenfeng County	贞丰县	314,785	303,883	-10,902	-3.46	292,981	3,340	5,789	9,129	724	1,447	2,171	11,300	3.86
		2,864,920	2,804,612	-60,308	-2.11	2,744,304	31,793	55,107	86,900	6,778	13,557	20,335	107,235	3.91
Tongren Prefecture	铜仁市													
Bijiang District	碧江区	308,583	361,670	53,087	17.20	414,757	5,558	9,633	15,191	1,024	2,049	3,073	18,264	4.40
Dejiang County	德江县	388,639	367,920	-20,719	-5.33	347,201	4,652	8,064	12,717	858	1,715	2,573	15,289	4.40
Jiangkou County	江口县	189,288	172,761	-16,527	-8.73	156,234	2,094	3,629	5,722	386	772	1,158	6,880	4.40
Shiqian County	石阡县	334,508	304,387	-30,121	-9.00	274,266	3,675	6,370	10,045	677	1,355	2,032	12,078	4.40
Sinan County	思南县	543,389	499,336	-44,053	-8.11	455,283	6,101	10,575	16,675	1,125	2,249	3,374	20,049	4.40
Songtao County	松桃苗族自治县	547,488	486,748	-60,740	-11.09	426,008	5,709	9,895	15,603	1,052	2,104	3,157	18,760	4.40
Wanshan District	万山区	54,674	47,818	-6,856	-12.54	40,962	549	951	1,500	101	202	304	1,804	4.40
Yanhe County	沿河土家族自治县	474,331	449,819	-24,512	-5.17	425,307	5,699	9,878	15,577	1,051	2,101	3,152	18,729	4.40
Yinjiang County	印江土家族苗族自治县	335,263	284,220	-51,043	-15.22	233,177	3,125	5,416	8,540	576	1,152	1,728	10,268	4.40
Yuping County	玉屏侗族自治县	126,462	118,525	-7,937	-6.28	110,588	1,482	2,569	4,050	273	546	819	4,870	4.40
		3,302,625	3,093,204	-209,421	-6.34	2,883,783	38,643	66,979	105,622	7,123	14,246	21,369	126,991	4.40
Zunyi Prefecture	遵义市													
Bozhou District	播州区	1,243,193	942,904	-300,289	-24.15	642,615	5,655	9,802	15,457	1,587	3,175	4,762	20,219	3.15
Chishui City	赤水市	251,780	237,052	-14,728	-5.85	222,324	4,891	8,478	13,369	549	1,098	1,647	15,016	6.75
Daozhen County	道真仡佬族苗族自治县	286,715	244,159	-42,556	-14.84	201,603	1,774	3,075	4,849	498	996	1,494	6,343	3.15
Fenggang County	凤冈县	370,253	313,128	-57,125	-15.43	256,003	2,253	3,905	6,158	632	1,265	1,897	8,055	3.15
Honghuagang Distict	红花岗区	656,592	656,592	0	0.00	656,592	5,778	10,015	15,793	1,622	3,244	4,865	20,658	3.15
Huichuan District	汇川区	438,279	438,279	0	0.00	438,279	3,857	6,685	10,542	1,083	2,165	3,248	13,790	3.15
Meitan County	湄潭县	411,613	377,358	-34,255	-8.32	343,103	3,019	5,233	8,253	847	1,695	2,542	10,795	3.15
Renhuai City	仁怀市	520,759	546,477	25,718	4.94	572,195	11,444	19,836	31,280	1,413	2,827	4,240	35,520	6.21
Suiyang County	绥阳县	457,104	380,083	-77,021	-16.85	303,062	2,667	4,623	7,290	749	1,497	2,246	9,535	3.15
Tongzi County	桐梓县	575,580	521,840	-53,740	-9.34	468,100	4,119	7,140	11,259	1,156	2,312	3,469	14,728	3.15
Wuchuan County	务川仡佬族苗族自治县	386,164	321,657	-64,507	-16.70	257,150	2,263	3,922	6,185	635	1,270	1,905	8,091	3.15
Xishui County	习水县	591,208	523,180	-68,028	-11.51	455,152	4,005	6,942	10,948	1,124	2,248	3,373	14,320	3.15
Yuqing County	余庆县	252,965	234,739	-18,226	-7.20	216,513	1,905	3,302	5,208	535	1,070	1,604	6,812	3.15
Zheng'an County	正安县	504,832	389,634	-115,198	-22.82	274,436	2,415	4,186	6,601	678	1,356	2,034	8,635	3.15
		6,543,860	6,127,082	-819,955	-12.53	5,307,127	56,046	97,144	153,190	13,109	26,217	39,326	192,516	3.63
Totals		35,247,695	34,748,556	-499,139	-1.42	34,249,417	944,930	1,637,847	2,582,778	91,396	182,791	274,187	2,856,965	8.34

People groups in Guizhou

Groups primarily located in Guizhou Province
Latest statistics from <www.joshuaproject.net>

People group	Official nationality	Primary language	Primary religion	Population (all of China) 2018	All Christians	Percent	Evangelicals	Percent
A-Hmao	Miao	Miao, Big Flowery	Christianity	440,000	352,000	80.0	330,000	75.0
Ai-Cham	Bouyei	Ai-Cham	Animism	3,000	15	0.5	6	0.2
Aou	Gelao	Aou	Animism	2,730	0	0.0	0	0.0
Baheng, Liping	Yao	Baheng	Animism	6,500	0	0.0	0	0.0
Baheng, Sanjiang	Yao	Baheng	Animism	47,000	0	0.0	0	0.0
Baonuo	Yao	Bunu, Bunao	Animism	32,000	128	0.4	96	0.3
Beidongnuo	Yao	Miao, Northern Qiandong	Animism	500	0	0.0	0	0.0
Cai	Undetermined	Gelao, Green	Animism	33,000	990	3.0	825	2.5
Changpao	Yao	Bunu, Bunao	Animism	6,600	0	0.0	0	0.0
Chuanlan	Han	Chinese, Mandarin	Buddhism	386,000	28,950	7.5	26,248	6.8
Chuanqing	Undetermined	Chinese, Mandarin	Buddhism	978,000	73,350	7.5	66,504	6.8
Diao	Dong	Chinese, Mandarin	Animism	2,700	0	0.0	0	0.0
Dong, Northern	Dong	Dong, Northern	Animism	574,000	689	0.1	574	0.1
Dong, Southern	Dong	Dong, Southern	Animism	1,219,000	853	0.1	853	0.1
Duoluo	Gelao	Duluo	Animism	2,800	70	2.5	70	2.5
Ga Mong	She	Miao, Chuanqiandian	Animism	69,000	0	0.0	0	0.0
Gao	Gelao	Gelao, Green	Animism	3,500	263	7.5	238	6.8
Ge	Miao	Ge	Animism	132,000	158	0.1	132	0.1
Gelao	Gelao	Chinese, Mandarin	Animism	726,000	30,492	4.2	18,876	2.6
Gha-Mu	Miao	Miao, Small Flowery	Christianity	139,000	111,200	80.0	69,500	50.0
Gouzou	Yi	Nasu, Wusa	Animism	5,200	260	5.0	254	4.9
Guopu	Yi	Nasu, Wusa	Animism	109,000	21,800	20.0	19,620	18.0
Hagei	Gelao	Gelao, Red	Animism	3,000	0	0.0	0	0.0
Hmong Be	Miao	Hua Miao	Animism	1,300	0	0.0	0	0.0
Hmong Dou	Miao	Hua Miao	Animism	4,100	451	11.0	388	9.5
Hmong Shua	Miao	Sinicized Miao	Animism	344,000	8,600	2.5	6,192	1.8
Hmu, Eastern	Miao	Miao, Qiandong	Animism	579,000	17,370	3.0	1,274	0.2
Hmu, Northern	Miao	Miao, Qiandong	Animism	2,041,000	6,123	0.3	5,103	0.3
Hmu, Southern	Miao	Miao, Qiandong	Animism	827,000	1,654	0.2	496	0.1
Laba	Miao	Chinese, Mandarin	Animism	293,000	879	0.3	645	0.2
Lagou	Yi	Nasu, Wusa	Animism	7,700	2,695	35.0	2,695	35.0
Limin	Yi	Chinese, Mandarin	Animism	98,000	147	0.2	127	0.1
Liujia	Han	Chinese, Mandarin	Animism	4,800	0	0.0	0	0.0
Longjia	Bai	Chinese, Mandarin	Animism	4,000	180	4.5	152	3.8
Lu	Manchu	Chinese, Mandarin	Animism	6,000	0	0.0	0	0.0
Miao, Baishi	Miao	Chinese, Mandarin	Animism	17,000	0	0.0	0	0.0
Miao, Changshu	Miao	Miao, Chuanqiandian	Animism	20,000	680	3.4	380	1.9

People group	Official nationality	Primary language	Primary religion	Population (all of China) 2018	All Christians	Percent	Evangelicals	Percent
Miao, Guiyang (Northern)	Miao	Miao, Guiyang	Animism	140,000	1,400	1.0	1,260	0.9
Miao, Guiyang (Northwestern)	Miao	Miao, Guiyang	Animism	9,900	0	0.0	0	0.0
Miao, Guiyang (South Central)	Miao	Miao, Guiyang	Animism	5,800	0	0.0	0	0.0
Miao, Guiyang (Southeastern)	Miao	Miao, Guiyang	Animism	117,000	11,700	10.0	10,530	9.0
Miao, Guiyang (Southern)	Miao	Miao, Guiyang	Animism	46,000	4,600	10.0	4,140	9.0
Miao, Horned	Miao	Miao, Horned	Animism	82,000	4,264	5.2	4,100	5.0
Miao, Hua	Miao	Miao, Chuanqiandian	Animism	767,000	1,534	0.2	1,304	0.2
Miao, Huishui (Central)	Miao	Miao, Huishui	Animism	66,000	660	1.0	383	0.6
Miao, Huishui (Eastern)	Miao	Miao, Huishui	Animism	23,000	115	0.5	64	0.3
Miao, Huishui (Northern)	Miao	Miao, Huishui	Animism	117,000	1,170	1.0	70	0.1
Miao, Huishui (Southwestern)	Miao	Miao, Huishui	Animism	94,000	0	0.0	0	0.0
Miao, Liupanshui	Miao	Chinese, Xiang	Animism	66,000	2,640	4.0	1,320	2.0
Miao, Luobohe	Miao	Miao, Luobohe	Animism	100,000	0	0.0	0	0.0
Miao, Mashan (Central)	Miao	Miao, Mashan	Animism	118,000	1,180	1.0	295	0.3
Miao, Mashan (Northern)	Miao	Miao, Mashan	Animism	58,000	0	0.0	0	0.0
Miao, Mashan (Southern)	Miao	Miao, Mashan	Animism	17,000	0	0.0	0	0.0
Miao, Mashan (Western)	Miao	Miao, Mashan	Animism	23,000	0	0.0	0	0.0
Mjuniang	Miao	Cao Miao	Animism	55,000	0	0.0	0	0.0
Mo	Bouyei	Mak	Animism	14,000	28	0.2	22	0.2
Mulao Jia	Undetermined	Chinese, Mandarin	Animism	39,000	0	0.0	0	0.0
Nanjingren	Bai	Chinese, Mandarin	Buddhism	159,000	11,925	7.5	10,812	6.8
Nasu, Panxian	Yi	Nasu, Wusa	Animism	366,000	7,320	2.0	6,295	1.7
Nasu, Wusa	Yi	Nasu, Wumeng	Animism	314,000	94,200	30.0	75,800	24.1
Nosu, Shuixi	Yi	Nasu, Wusa	Animism	298,000	8,940	3.0	7,152	2.4
Numao	Yao	Bunu, Bunao	Animism	2,300	0	0.0	0	0.0
Qanu	Miao	Miao, Qiandong	Animism	15,000	0	0.0	0	0.0
Qixingmin	Bai	Chinese, Mandarin	Buddhism	5,800	0	0.0	0	0.0
Rao	Yao & Bouyei	Rao	Animism	13,000	0	0.0	0	0.0
Sanqiao	Miao & Dong	Dong, Southern	Animism	6,700	0	0.0	0	0.0
Shenzhou	Han	Chinese, Mandarin	Buddhism	4,800	202	4.2	182	3.8
Shui	Shui	Shui	Animism	321,000	899	0.3	803	0.3
Tushu	Yi	Nasu, Wusa	Animism	6,500	650	10.0	514	7.9
Wopu	Yi	Nasu, Wusa	Animism	3,900	0	0.0	0	0.0
Xi	She	Miao, Luobohe	Animism	1,700	0	0.0	0	0.0
Xialusi	Dong	Chinese, Mandarin	Animism	3,900	0	0.0	0	0.0
Yanghuang	Maonan	T'en	Animism	15,000	0	0.0	0	0.0
Yizi	Gelao	Chinese, Mandarin	Animism	2,900	0	0.0	0	0.0
Youmai	Yao	Iu Mien	Animism	2,700	0	0.0	0	0.0
Totals				12,667,330	813,423	6.4	676,293	5.3

Notes

The China Chronicles overview

1 R. Wardlaw Thompson, *Griffith John: The Story of Fifty Years in China* (London: The Religious Tract Society, 1908), p. 65.

Introduction

1 Lijia Zhang, "One in 60 Million: Life as a 'Left-Behind' Child in China," *South China Morning Post* (January 21, 2018).
2 Rob Schmitz, "Xi Jinping's War on Poverty Moves Millions of Chinese off the Farm": <www.npr.org> (October 19, 2017).
3 Harrison E. Salisbury, *The Long March: The Untold Story* (London: Macmillan, 1985). The dire poverty had changed little by the time the author personally visited areas of southern Guizhou in the early 1990s, where the inhabitants were so poor they literally walked around naked and in distress, despite the cold weather. Families were so bound by poverty that they didn't possess any clothing at all.
4 Marco Polo, *The Travels of Marco Polo: The Complete Yule-Cordier Edition*, Vol. 2 (New York: Dover, 1903), p. 124.
5 Polo, *The Travels of Marco Polo*, Vol. 2, p. 124.
6 Polo, *The Travels of Marco Polo*, Vol. 2, pp. 124–6.
7 See the table "People groups in Guizhou" in the Appendix of this book for a full list of all groups in the province.
8 Shunsheng Ling and Yihfu Ruey, "A Report on the Investigation of the Miao of Western Hunan," *Academia Sinica* (Shanghai, 1947), pp. 165–8.
9 Paul Hattaway, *Operation China: Introducing All the Peoples of China* (Carlisle: Piquant, 2000), p. 205.
10 *Chinese Recorder and Missionary Journal* (January 1884), p. 51.
11 "A Narrow Escape from Death: Mountain Trail Perils Faced by Evangelists," *China News and Church Report* (April 24, 1992).
12 *Bridge* (July–August 1987).

The mysterious origins of the Miao

1 Keith Quincy, *Hmong: A History of a People* (Cheney, WA: Eastern Washington University Press, 1995), p. 18.

2 Mike and Melissa Miao, "The Miao of China," an unpublished prayer guide, Hong Kong, 1994.
3 Quincy, *Hmong*, pp. 18–20.
4 Quincy, *Hmong*, p. 25.
5 "In eastern Guizhou a young Miao girl invited me home with her. I shared the Good News, and she translated it into her Miao dialect for her mother. When I got to the part [where] God had created man from the dirt, and then made woman from one of his bones, the mother got all excited. 'Listen to her. Whatever she tells you, it is true!' she exclaimed. 'We Miao also have this story.' The teenager came to Christ that night, and several from her family also soon after." Personal communication with a missionary to the Miao, March 2017.
6 Edgar A. Truax, "Genesis According to the Miao People," *Impact: Institute for Creation Research* (April 1991). Used by kind permission of the Institute for Creation Research.

Early Christian martyrs

1 Nicolas Standaert, *Handbook of Christianity in China, Volume One: 635–1800* (Leiden: Brill, 2001), p. 386.
2 Chinese Regional Bishops' Conference (CRBC), *The Newly Canonized Martyr-Saints of China* (Taiwan: CRBC September 8th Editorial Board, 2000), p. 3.
3 CRBC, *The Newly Canonized Martyr-Saints of China*, p. 9.
4 CRBC, *The Newly Canonized Martyr-Saints of China*, p. 9.
5 CRBC, *The Newly Canonized Martyr-Saints of China*, p. 9.
6 CRBC, *The Newly Canonized Martyr-Saints of China*, pp. 16–17.
7 CRBC, *The Newly Canonized Martyr-Saints of China*, p. 18.
8 CRBC, *The Newly Canonized Martyr-Saints of China*, p. 19.
9 CRBC, *The Newly Canonized Martyr-Saints of China*, pp. 18–20.
10 "The Martyrs of China 1648–1930," *Tripod* (September–October 2000), p. 27.
11 CRBC, *The Newly Canonized Martyr-Saints of China*, pp. 90–1.
12 *China's Millions* (October 1875), p. 43.

1870s and 1880s

1 "Wild Tribes in China," *China's Millions* (November 1875), p. 50.
2 "Province of Kwei-chau," *China's Millions* (August 1877), p. 92.
3 "Province of Kwei-chau," p. 92.
4 Chas. H. Judd, "Journey through Hunan, Kweichow and Szechuen Provinces," *Chinese Recorder and Missionary Journal* (November 1887), p. 507.

5 Judd, "Journey through Hunan, Kweichow and Szechuen Provinces," p. 508.
6 J. F. Broumton, "Work in Kwei-yang," *China's Millions* (February 1878), p. 28.
7 Charlotte Kerr, "Women's Work in Kwei-chau, Western China," *China's Millions* (December 1881), p. 145.
8 Miss Kidd, "Making Friends at Kwei-yang Fu," *China's Millions* (February 1882), p. 15.
9 Kidd, "Making Friends at Kwei-yang Fu," p. 15.
10 Kidd, "Making Friends at Kwei-yang Fu," p. 20.
11 "The Kwei-chau Christians," *China's Millions* (February 1896), p. 20.
12 "The Kwei-chau Christians," p. 20.
13 *China's Millions* (July 1888), p. 84.
14 *China's Millions* (May 1887), p. 86.
15 *China's Millions* (August 1890), p. 102.
16 *Chinese Recorder and Missionary Journal* (March 1890).

1890s

1 American Presbyterian Mission, *The China Mission Handbook* (Shanghai: American Presbyterian Mission Press, 1896), p. 145.
2 *China's Millions* (September 1886), p. 122.
3 Samuel R. Clarke, *Among the Tribes in South-West China* (London: Morgan & Scott, 1911), p. 144.
4 Clarke, *Among the Tribes in South-West China*, pp. 156–7.
5 Clarke, *Among the Tribes in South-West China*, p. 159.

The Hmu

1 "Among the Miao-tsi," *China's Millions* (February 1897), p. 12.
2 See Paul Hattaway, *Operation China: Introducing All the Peoples of China* (Carlisle: Piquant, 2000), for profiles of 490 distinct ethno-linguistic groups in China, including more than 40 groups that comprise the official Miao nationality.
3 S. R. Clarke, "P'an, the Evangelist," *China's Millions* (August 1899), p. 121.
4 Clarke, "P'an, the Evangelist," p. 121.
5 Samuel R. Clarke, *Among the Tribes in South-West China* (London: Morgan & Scott, 1911), pp. 163–4.
6 J. R. Adam, "Persecution of the Black Miao in Kwei-chau," *China's Millions* (January 1902), p. 11.
7 Adam, "Persecution of the Black Miao," p. 11.

8 The exact number of Hmu Christians put to death is unclear. Some sources gave the total number as 32, but J. R. Adam's account seems the most detailed, and stated there were 34 Christians or Christian inquirers killed. See Adam, "Persecution of the Black Miao," pp. 11–12.

9 Adam, "Persecution of the Black Miao," pp. 11–12.

10 M. H. Hutton, "'In Journeyings' amongst the Miao," *China's Millions* (June 1914), pp. 47–8.

11 M. H. Hutton, "How the Message Came to the Black Miao," *China's Millions* (November 1937), p. 214.

12 M. H. Hutton, "Encouraging Results and Discouraging Circumstances," an unpublished circular letter, 1927.

13 "Among the Miao," *China's Millions* (September 1927), p. 140.

14 "The Black Miao," *China's Millions* (April 1928), p. 55.

15 M. H. Hutton, "Among the Black Miao," *China's Millions* (March 1932), p. 49.

16 Hutton, "How the Message Came," p. 214.

17 Hutton, "Among the Black Miao," p. 49.

18 M. H. Hutton, "Safely Back in Panghai," *China's Millions* (March 1930), p. 91.

19 Joakim Enwall, *A Myth Become Reality: History and Development of the Miao Written Language*, Vol. 1 (Stockholm: Institute of Oriental Languages, 1996), p. 216.

20 *The Field Bulletin of the China Inland Mission* (April 1950), pp. 56–7.

21 Ivan Allbutt, "The Black Miao of Kweichow," *China's Millions* (October 1950), p. 106.

22 See the table "People groups in Guizhou" in the Appendix of this book. The Hmu in Guizhou are divided into three dialect groups, designated Northern, Eastern and Southern Hmu.

1900s

1 Mr. Windsor, "Encouragement in Kwei-yang," *China's Millions* (October 1902), p. 140.

2 *China's Millions* (July–August 1903), p. 105.

3 Charles T. Fishe, "Brief Notes of a Journey to Tu-shan, Kwei-chau," *China's Millions* (April 1903), p. 46.

4 J. Hudson Taylor, "In Memoriam—Mrs. Adam," *China's Millions* (February 1895), p. 8.

5 Taylor, "In Memoriam—Mrs. Adam," pp. 8–9.

6 James Adam married his first wife (whose maiden name was Haynes) in 1893, his second wife Harriet in 1897, and his third wife (whose maiden name was E. M. S. Anderson) in 1904.

7 Joakim Enwall, *A Myth Become Reality: History and Development of the Miao Written Language*, Vol. 1 (Stockholm: Institute of Oriental Languages, 1996), p. 94.

8 Enwall, *A Myth Become Reality*, p. 57.

9 Enwall, *A Myth Become Reality*, p. 95.

10 William H. Hudspeth, *Stone-Gateway and the Flowery Miao* (London: Cargate Press, 1937), pp. 38–9.

11 *China's Millions* (February 1906), p. 33.

12 J. R. Adam, "Pentecostal Blessing among the Aborigines of West China," *China's Millions* (January 1907), p. 11.

13 Adam, "Pentecostal Blessing," p. 11.

14 Adam, "Pentecostal Blessing," pp. 11–12.

15 Jasper Becker, "Church Planting Past and Present," *Pray for China* (May–June 1996), p. 2.

16 Adam, "Pentecostal Blessing," p. 12.

17 Adam, "Pentecostal Blessing," p. 13.

18 Samuel Pollard, *The Story of the Miao* (London: Henry Books, 1919), pp. 47–8.

19 *China's Millions* (February 1906), p. 33.

20 Adam, "Pentecostal Blessing," p. 14.

21 Adam, "Pentecostal Blessing," p. 14.

22 Adam, "Pentecostal Blessing," p. 14.

23 Adam, "Pentecostal Blessing," pp. 28–30.

24 G. Cecil-Smith, "The Work in Kweiyang District," *China's Millions* (July 1909), p. 101.

25 American Presbyterian Mission, *The China Mission Handbook* (Shanghai: American Presbyterian Mission Press, 1896), p. 145.

26 *China's Millions* (November 1905).

27 "A Tour amongst the Miao Villages," *China's Millions* (February 1909), p. 26.

28 Enwall, *A Myth Become Reality*, p. 98.

29 "A Tour amongst the Miao Villages," p. 30.

1910s

1 James R. Adam, "A Tour among the Aborigines in Kweichow," *China's Millions* (December 1912), p. 184.

2 Samuel L. Clarke, *Among the Tribes in South-West China* (London: Morgan & Scott, 1911), pp. 248–9.

3 By 1949 it was estimated that 34,500 people used the A-Hmao New Testament in the Pollard script, while only 5,000 still used the Roman

script developed by James Adam. See Joakim Enwall, *A Myth Become Reality: History and Development of the Miao Written Language*, Vol. 1 (Stockholm: Institute of Oriental Languages, 1996), p. 216.

4 James R. Adam, "Progress and Promise among the Aborigines," *China's Millions* (September 1911), p. 137.

5 W. H. Hudspeth, "A Miao Quarterly Meeting," *The West China Missionary News* (January 1917), p. 13.

6 J. R. Adam, "The Tribespeople of Kweichow," *China's Millions* (January 1914), p. 13.

7 J. R. Adam, "Another Tour among the Tribespeople," *China's Millions* (February 1914), p. 29.

8 Edward S. Fish, "A Medical Tour among the Aborigines," *China's Millions* (October 1914), p. 155.

9 Fish, "A Medical Tour among the Aborigines," p. 155.

10 Fish, "A Medical Tour among the Aborigines," p. 157.

11 Fish, "A Medical Tour among the Aborigines," p. 158.

12 Adam, "Another Tour among the Tribespeople," pp. 27–8.

13 "In Memoriam: J. R. Adam and Thomas Windsor," *China's Millions* (October 1915), p. 160.

14 Ralph R. Covell, *The Liberating Gospel in China: The Christian Faith among China's Minority Peoples* (Grand Rapids, MI: Baker Book House, 1995), pp. 93–4.

15 "Letter of Sympathy to Mrs. Adam by Two Miao Christians," *China's Millions* (January 1916), p. 4.

16 William H. Hudspeth, *Stone-Gateway and the Flowery Miao* (London: Cargate Press, 1937), p. 41.

17 A 1919 figure cited in Milton T. Stauffer (ed.), *The Christian Occupation of China* (Shanghai: China Continuation Committee, 1922), p. 183.

18 Only 9,446 of these believers were "communicant" Christians at the time, meaning baptized church members in good standing who were permitted to take communion.

19 Bertram Wolferstan, *The Catholic Church in China from 1860 to 1907* (London: Sands & Co., 1909), p. 450.

20 Stauffer, *The Christian Occupation of China*, p. 181.

1920s

1 "Among the Miao," *China's Millions* (September 1927), p. 140.

2 D. V. Rees, "Among the Tribes," *China's Millions* (March 1928), p. 46.

3 Morris S. Slichter, "Itinerating among the Miao," *China's Millions* (October 1926), p. 154.

4 Slichter, "Itinerating among the Miao," p. 156.
5 "In Perils of Robbers," *China's Millions* (July 1927), p. 110.
6 Mrs. J. Yorkston, "Answered Prayer," *China's Millions* (November 1929), p. 173.
7 Milton T. Stauffer (ed.), *The Christian Occupation of China* (Shanghai: China Continuation Committee, 1922), pp. 179–81.
8 Stauffer, *The Christian Occupation of China*, pp. 179–80.
9 J. H. Robinson, "An Appeal from Kweichow," *China's Millions* (November 1934), p. 208.
10 H. L. Taylor, "The Work in Our District," *China's Millions* (July 1931), p. 126.

1930s

1 *China's Millions* (June 1931), p. 109.
2 H. L. Taylor, "Wengan, Kweichow," *China's Millions* (September 1932), p. 175.
3 A. Hayman, "Kiuchow, Kweichow," *China's Millions* (January 1933), p. 8.
4 J. Edwin Orr, *Evangelical Awakenings in Eastern Asia* (Minneapolis, MN: Bethany House, 1975), p. 90.
5 E. A. Crapuchettes, "Revival in Kweichow," *China's Millions* (May 1934), p. 84.
6 C. E. Chapman, "The Tide Has Turned," *China's Millions* (November 1934), p. 209.
7 Crapuchettes, "Revival in Kweichow," pp. 85–6.
8 M. H. Hutton, "The New Testament for the Black Miao," *China's Millions* (November 1935), p. 205.
9 M. H. Hutton, "How the Message Came to the Black Miao," *China's Millions* (November 1937), p. 214.
10 Joakim Enwall, *A Myth Become Reality: History and Development of the Miao Written Language*, Vol. 1 (Stockholm: Institute of Oriental Languages, 1996), p. 159.
11 "Prisoners of Jesus Christ," *China's Millions* (May 1935), p. 100.
12 R. A. Bosshardt, *The Restraining Hand: Captivity for Christ in China* (London: Hodder & Stoughton, 1936), p. 120.
13 Bosshardt, *The Restraining Hand*, pp. 251–2.
14 "The Release of Mr. Bosshardt," *China's Millions* (June 1936), pp. 105–6.

1940s

1 C. G. Edwards, "Kweichow Tribal Report," *The Field Bulletin of the China Inland Mission* (November 1948), p. 195.

2 R. J. R. Butler, "The Lord's Work Is Costly," *China's Millions* (January–February 1948), p. 8.

3 Leslie Lyall, "The Passing Crowd," *China's Millions* (September–October 1943), p. 37.

4 J. Howard Kitchen, "Kweichow Province: A Survey," *China's Millions* (July–August 1945), p. 29.

5 Sister M. C. Welzel, "The Friedenshort Deaconess Mission," *China's Millions* (November 1933), p. 206.

6 Sister M. Welzel, "In the Wake of a Mass Movement," *China's Millions* (December 1937), p. 233.

7 Welzel, "In the Wake of a Mass Movement," p. 234.

8 *China's Millions* (May 1936), p. 96.

9 Muriel Rae, *His Banner Over Us Is Love* (self-published book, 1995), p. 158.

10 Rae, *His Banner Over Us Is Love*, pp. 159–60.

11 Kitchen, "Kweichow Province," p. 30.

12 P. K. Parsons, unpublished manuscript, cited in Joakim Enwall, *A Myth Become Reality: History and Development of the Miao Written Language*, Vol. 1 (Stockholm: Institute of Oriental Languages, 1996), p. 136.

13 Parsons, cited in Enwall, *A Myth Become Reality*, p. 136.

14 Parsons, cited in Enwall, *A Myth Become Reality*, p. 136.

15 *Bridge* (July–August 1987).

16 Milton T. Stauffer (ed.), *The Christian Occupation of China* (Shanghai: China Continuation Committee, 1922), p. 183.

17 Taken from individual diocese figures published at <www.catholic-hierarchy.org>.

The Nosu

1 Samuel L. Clarke, *Among the Tribes in South-West China* (London: Morgan & Scott, 1911), p. 129.

2 R. Elliot Kendall, *Eyes of the Earth: The Diary of Samuel Pollard* (London: Cargate Press, 1954), p. 147.

3 Clarke, *Among the Tribes in South-West China*, p. 121.

4 Kendall, *Eyes of the Earth*, p. 90.

5 Kendall, *Eyes of the Earth*, p. 120.

6 Clarke, *Among the Tribes in South-West China*, pp. 123–4.

7 James R. Adam, "Progress and Promise among the Aborigines," *China's Millions* (September 1911), p. 137.

8 J. R. Adam, "A Year's Work at Anshunfu," *China's Millions* (May 1915), pp. 77–8.

9 Isaac Page, "Further Blessing among the Miao," *China's Millions* (February 1918), p. 20.

10 Milton T. Stauffer (ed.), *The Christian Occupation of China* (Shanghai: China Continuation Committee, 1922), p. 182.

11 "New Churches, Ordinations for Yi Christians," *Amity News Service* (April 1993).

12 Linda Baker Kaahanui, *Every Good Gift: Sufficient Grace in Time of Need* (Fort Washington, PA: Christian Literature Crusade, 1999), pp. 80–1.

13 Kaahanui, *Every Good Gift*, p. 82.

14 Kaahanui, *Every Good Gift*, p. 83.

15 Tony Lambert, *China's Christian Millions: The Costly Revival* (London: Monarch, 1999), pp. 213–14.

1950s and 1960s

1 Leslie T. Lyall, *A Passion for the Impossible: The China Inland Mission 1865–1965* (London: Hodder & Stoughton, 1965), p. 162.

2 Margery Sykes, "A Spiritual Battle, Fought and Won," *China's Millions* (February 1951), p. 18.

3 J. Howard Kitchen, "Kweichow Province: A Survey," *China's Millions* (July–August 1945), p. 30.

4 *China's Millions* (March 1951), p. 1.

5 Carl Lawrence with David Wang, *The Coming Influence of China* (Sisters, OR: Multnomah, 1996), pp. 30–1.

6 Lawrence, *The Coming Influence of China*, p. 31.

7 Tony Lambert, *China's Christian Millions: The Costly Revival* (London: Monarch, 1999), pp. 99–100.

8 Lambert, *China's Christian Millions*, p. 101.

1970s

1 Leslie T. Lyall, *New Spring in China? A Christian Appraisal* (London: Hodder & Stoughton, 1979), p. 192.

2 Lyall, *New Spring in China?*, pp. 192–3.

3 Tony Lambert, *China's Christian Millions: The Costly Revival* (London: Monarch, 1999), p. 100.

4 Joakim Enwall, *A Myth Become Reality: History and Development of the Miao Written Language*, Vol. 1 (Stockholm: Institute of Oriental Languages, 1996), p. 217.

5 Lambert, *China's Christian Millions*, pp. 101–2.

1980s

1 Wong Tak Hing, "A Pilgrimage to the Mountains: A Visit to Miao Churches in Guizhou Province," *Bridge* (July–August 1987), pp. 9–10.
2 Tony Lambert, *China's Christian Millions: The Costly Revival* (London: Monarch, 1999), pp. 104–5.
3 Ralph R. Covell, *The Liberating Gospel in China: The Christian Faith among China's Minority Peoples* (Grand Rapids, MI: Baker Book House, 1995), p. 92.
4 Joakim Enwall, *A Myth Become Reality: History and Development of the Miao Written Language*, Vol. 1 (Stockholm: Institute of Oriental Languages, 1996), p. 217.
5 Peter Xu Yongze, personal communication, October 2003.
6 "A Narrow Escape from Death," *China News and Church Report* (April 24, 1992).
7 Leslie T. Lyall, *The Phoenix Rises: The Phenomenal Growth of Eight Chinese Churches* (Singapore: Overseas Missionary Fellowship, 1992), p. 145.
8 Marjorie K. Baker, "What Makes China's Church Grow?", *Asian Report* (March–April 1989), pp. 9–10.
9 Baker, "What Makes China's Church Grow?", p. 11.
10 Paul E. Kauffman, *Piecing Together the China Puzzle* (Hong Kong: Asian Outreach, 1987), p. 153.
11 Far East Broadcasting, February 1989.
12 *Bridge* (July–August 1987).

The Bouyei

1 Samuel R. Clarke, *Among the Tribes in South-West China* (London: Morgan & Scott, 1911), pp. 97–9.
2 S. R. Clarke, "The Aborigines of Kwei-chau," *China's Millions* (April 1903), p. 47.
3 Clarke, *Among the Tribes in South-West China*, p. 107.
4 Clarke, "The Aborigines of Kwei-chau," p. 47.
5 Clarke, *Among the Tribes in South-West China*, pp. 152–3.
6 Morris Slichter, "New Centres Visited among the Aborigines," *China's Millions* (October 1919), p. 115.
7 J. H. Robinson, "An Appeal from Kweichow," *China's Millions* (November 1934), p. 209.
8 Cyril G. Edwards, "Glimpses of Tribal Survey," *China's Millions* (March–April 1948), p. 19.
9 David Joannes, *The Space between Memories: Recollections from a 21st*

Century Missionary (Prescott, AZ: Within Reach Global, 2016), pp. 180–1.

10 Frontier Harvest Ministries, December 2008.
11 Frontier Harvest Ministries, August 2010.

1990s

1 *Ming Bao* (August 31, 1995), cited in Tony Lambert, *China's Christian Millions: The Costly Revival* (London: Monarch, 1999), p. 145.
2 Jasper Becker, "Church Planting Past and Present," *Pray for China* (May–June 1996), p. 2.
3 Becker, "Church Planting Past and Present," p. 3.
4 Lambert, *China's Christian Millions*, pp. 213–14.
5 Global Chinese Ministries, December 1998.
6 *Pray for China* (July–August 1999).
7 *Weining Yizu Huizu Miaozu Zizhixian Minzuzhi* [The Annals of the Minority Nationalities of the Weining Yi, Hui and Miao Autonomous County], 1997, p. 128.
8 *Bridge* (July–August 1987).

2000s

1 Mark Kelley, "God Is at Work among the Miao of China," *IMB News* (December 6, 2002).
2 Kelley, "God Is at Work among the Miao of China."
3 Kelley, "God Is at Work among the Miao of China."
4 Luke Wesley, *Stories from China: Fried Rice for the Soul* (Waynesboro, GA: Authentic, 2005), pp. 25–6.
5 *China Testimonies*, privately circulated newsletter, September 2005.
6 Bob Fu, "Martyred in China," *The Voice of the Martyrs* (March 2005), p. 6.
7 Fu, "Martyred in China," p. 6.
8 China Aid Association, "Call for Justice": <www.chinaaid.org>.
9 Wesley, *Stories from China*, pp. 97–8.
10 Personal communication, January 6, 2003.
11 Frontier Harvest Ministries, December 2001.
12 Far East Broadcasting, October 2001.
13 Patrick Johnstone and Jason Mandryk, *Operation World: 21st Century Edition* (Carlisle: Paternoster Lifestyle, 2001), p. 171.
14 Jason Mandryk, *Operation World: The Definitive Prayer Guide to Every Nation* (Colorado Springs, CO: Biblica, 2010), p. 234.
15 *Lift Up Our Holy Hands* (December 2000).

16 *Pray for China* (April–May 2000).
17 *Lift Up Our Holy Hands* (November 2000).
18 Far East Broadcasting, February 2001.
19 Far East Broadcasting, February 2001.
20 Far East Broadcasting, February 2001.
21 Far East Broadcasting, October 2001.
22 *Pray for China* (December 2001 – January 2002).
23 *Pray for China* (October–November 2001).
24 *Pray for China* (December 2003 – January 2004).
25 *Pray for China* (June–July 2003).
26 *Pray for China* (June–July 2005).
27 *Lift Up Our Holy Hands* (July 2005).
28 *Pray for China* (October–November 2006).
29 *Pray for China* (February–March 2009).
30 *Pray for China* (December 2009 – January 2010).

The Dong

1 Leslie T. Lyall, *Come Wind, Come Weather: The Present Experience of the Church in China* (London: Hodder & Stoughton, 1961), p. 85.
2 It is unclear how much use the Southern Dong New Testament has enjoyed, as few Dong people were taught to read the script. Most Dong believers probably use the Chinese Bible today.
3 Frontier Harvest Ministries, December 2009.
4 Frontier Harvest Ministries, May 2013.

2010s

1 China Aid Association, September 9, 2013.
2 China Aid Association, July 1, 2014.
3 China Aid Association, June 2, 2015.
4 China Aid Association, July 14, 2016.
5 Personal communication, November 2016.
6 China Aid Association, August 4, 2016.

Selected bibliography

American Presbyterian Mission, *The China Mission Handbook* (Shanghai: American Presbyterian Mission Press, 1896).

Bosshardt, R. A., *The Restraining Hand: Captivity for Christ in China* (London: Hodder & Stoughton, 1936).

Broomhall, A. J., *Hudson Taylor and China's Open Century: Book Six—Assault on the Nine* (London: Overseas Missionary Fellowship, 1988).

——, *Strong Tower* (London: China Inland Mission, 1947).

Broomhall, Marshall, *By Love Compelled: The Call of the China Inland Mission* (London: Hodder & Stoughton, 1936).

——, *Some a Hundredfold: The Life and Work of James R. Adam among the Tribes of South West China* (London: China Inland Mission, 1916).

Chinese Regional Bishops' Conference, *The Newly Canonized Martyr-Saints of China* (Taiwan: CRBC September 8th Editorial Board, 2000).

Clarke, Samuel R., *Among the Tribes in South-West China* (London: Morgan & Scott, 1911).

Covell, Ralph R., *The Liberating Gospel in China: The Christian Faith among China's Minority Peoples* (Grand Rapids, MI: Baker Book House, 1995).

Enwall, Joakim, *A Myth Become Reality: History and Development of the Miao Written Language*, Vol. 1 (Stockholm: Institute of Oriental Languages, 1996).

Grist, W. A., *Samuel Pollard: Pioneer Missionary in China* (London: Henry Books, 1920).

Hattaway, Paul, *Operation China: Introducing All the Peoples of China* (Carlisle: Piquant, 2000).

Hayes, Ernest H., *Sam Pollard of Yunnan* (London: The Pilgrim Press, 1928).

Herman, John E., *Amid the Clouds and Mist: China's Colonization of Guizhou, 1200–1700*, Harvard East Asian Monographs (Cambridge, MA: Harvard University Asia Center, 2007).

Hudspeth, William H., *Stone-Gateway and the Flowery Miao* (London: Cargate Press, 1937).

Jenks, Robert Darrah, *Insurgency and Social Disorder in Guizhou: The Miao Rebellion, 1854–1873* (Honolulu, HI: University of Hawaii Press, 1994).

Kaahanui, Linda Baker, *Every Good Gift: Sufficient Grace in Time of Need* (Fort Washington, PA: Christian Literature Crusade, 1999).

Kauffman, Paul E., *Piecing Together the China Puzzle* (Hong Kong: Asian Outreach, 1987).

——, *Through China's Open Door* (Hong Kong: Asian Outreach, 1979).

Kendall, R. Elliot, *Eyes of the Earth: The Diary of Samuel Pollard* (London: Cargate Press, 1954).

Lambert, Tony, *China's Christian Millions: The Costly Revival* (London: Monarch, 1999).

Lyall, Leslie T., *A Passion for the Impossible: The China Inland Mission 1865–1965* (London: Hodder & Stoughton, 1965).

——, *The Phoenix Rises: The Phenomenal Growth of Eight Chinese Churches* (Singapore: Overseas Missionary Fellowship, 1992).

Ma Yin, *China's Minority Nationalities* (Beijing: Foreign Languages Press, 1989).

Moody, Edward H., *Sam Pollard* (London: Oliphants, 1956).

Orr, J. Edwin, *Evangelical Awakenings in Eastern Asia* (Minneapolis, MN: Bethany House, 1975).

Pollard, Samuel, *The Story of the Miao* (London: Henry Books, 1919).

——, *Tight Corners in China* (London: A. Crombie, *c.*1911).

Pollard, Walter, *The Life of Sam Pollard of China: An Account of the Intrepid Life of Adventure, Danger, Toil and Travel* (London: Seeley, Service & Co., 1928).

Quincy, Keith, *Hmong: A History of a People* (Cheney, WA: Eastern Washington University Press, 1995).

Salisbury, Harrison E., *The Long March: The Untold Story* (London: Macmillan, 1985).

Stauffer, Milton T. (ed.), *The Christian Occupation of China* (Shanghai: China Continuation Committee, 1922).

Weinstein, Jodi L., *Empire and Identity in Guizhou: Local Resistance to Qing Expansion*, Studies on Ethnic Groups in China (Seattle, WA: University of Washington Press, 2013).

Wesley, Luke, *Stories from China: Fried Rice for the Soul* (Waynesboro, GA: Authentic, 2005).

Wolferstan, Bertram, *The Catholic Church in China from 1860 to 1907* (London: Sands & Co., 1909).

251

Contact details

Paul Hattaway is the founder and director of Asia Harvest, a non-denominational ministry that serves the Church in Asia through various strategic initiatives, including Bible printing and supporting Asian missionaries who share the gospel among unreached peoples.

The author can be reached by email at <**paul@asiaharvest. org**>, or by writing to him via any of the addresses listed below.

For more than 30 years Asia Harvest has served the Church in Asia through strategic projects that equip the local churches. At the time of going to print, Asia Harvest has successfully distributed more than 75,000 Bibles to house church Christians in Guizhou Province, in addition to supporting many evangelists among Guizhou's unreached people groups and providing aid to hundreds of persecuted church leaders and their families.

If you would like to receive the free Asia Harvest newsletter or to order other volumes in the China Chronicles series or Paul's other books, please visit <**www.asiaharvest.org**> or write to the address below nearest you:

Asia Harvest USA and Canada
353 Jonestown Rd #320
Winston-Salem, NC 27104
USA

Asia Harvest Australia
36 Nelson Street
Stepney, SA 5069
Australia

Asia Harvest New Zealand
PO Box 1757
Queenstown, 9348
New Zealand

Asia Harvest UK and Ireland
c/o AsiaLink
PO Box 891
Preston PR4 9AB
United Kingdom

Asia Harvest Europe
c/o Stiftung SALZ
Tailfinger Str. 28
71083 Herrenberg
Germany